Green Points:
The Definitive Guide

A Metric for the Maintenance and Remediation of Information Systems

Mel Small

FIRST EDITION

First published in paperback in 2019 by Sixth Element Publishing
on behalf of Mel Small

Sixth Element Publishing
Arthur Robinson House
13-14 The Green
Billingham
Stockton on Tees
TS23 1EU
Tel: 01642 360253
www.6epublishing.net

Copyright © 2019 by Mel Small

ISBN 978-1-912218-50-9

Copy editor/Proofreaders:
Susan Cunningham
David Forrest
Neil Hardy
Richard Shepherd

www.greenpts.org

Maintenance:
The act or process of preserving a condition or situation.

Remediation:
The act or process of rectifying something
that is undesirable or deficient.

Green Points:
A measure of the value embedded by the
maintenance and remediation of information systems.

Contents

Chapter 6 - Weighting Coefficients

Chapter 7 - Maintenance Life/Technology Count

Chapter 8 - Green Point Calculation

Chapter 9 - Applications of Green Point Analysis

Chapter 10 - System Health

Chapter 11 - Conclusion

Appendix A: Data Sheets

Appendix B: The Coffee Shop Example

Appendix C: Case Studies

Appendix D: Transaction Estimation

Appendix E: Other Weighting Coefficients

Appendix F: Frequently Asked Questions

Appendix G: Glossary of Terms

Chapter 1 - Introduction

Green Points: The Definitive Guide introduces the concept of Green Point Analysis, a method for understanding the value embedded by the maintenance and remediation of information systems. Green Point Analysis recognises that the work done by some systems is of greater business benefit than that done by others and provides a way of understanding and quantifying competing priorities. It does this by calculating green points.

A green point is a metric or unit of measurement used to express the value embedded by the maintenance and remediation of information systems. The calculation of a green point starts with the number of transactions processed by a system and applies weighting coefficients to reflect the business benefit delivered by those transactions.

This book describes the types of transactions that can be used in Green Point Analysis, the selection and application of weighting coefficients and the green point calculation. It discusses the practical applications of Green Point Analysis in both the upfront assessment of the benefits of maintenance and remediation activities, and the ongoing monitoring of the effectiveness of this work.

The concepts described in this book will help those responsible for the management of information systems make more informed decisions with respect to system maintenance.

Who Should Read This Book?

This book should be read by all those who have an interest in ensuring that the systems supporting their business are as well-maintained and robust as the available budget permits. This will include but is not limited to the following:

Systems analysts shaping maintenance activities who want to provide greater transparency with respect to the options available.

Portfolio, programme and project managers who would like to track project performance and progress using a metric other than cost.

Development managers wanting to monitor the incremental improvements following adjustments to the way maintenance work is undertaken.

Product owners looking to accommodate the competing priorities of business stakeholders.

Service owners responsible for ensuring the platforms they manage are stable and highly available.

Business sponsors wishing to ensure investment in maintenance and remediation activities is directed in the most efficient manner.

In summary, Green Point Analysis is of interest to all those who would like the money spent on maintenance and remediation activities to be directed in the most efficient manner possible.

What Do We Mean By Maintenance And Remediation?

To prevent confusion, it is worth defining what we mean by maintenance and remediation, and the type of activities that these terms encompass. Within this book and the context of Green Point Analysis, maintenance and remediation concern the non-functional upgrade of information systems. Primarily, this is the hardware, operating systems and middleware, such as servers, content management systems and messaging technology.

In addition, it may be valid to include application software under this banner. For example, if the implementation of a new version of a proprietary software package extends the vendor support period, it's hard to argue that this is much different to the upgrade of a server version with the same goal. Even the upgrade of bespoke application software, which adds functionality, can claim green points if it extends the support period past that provided by the previous version.

In Green Point Analysis, the difference between maintenance and remediation is subtle. Essentially, it concerns the timing of the activity being undertaken to upgrade the system. If the upgrade occurs while the system is still in support, it's maintenance; if support has expired, it's remediation. As mentioned at the start of this book, maintenance is the act or process of preserving a condition or situation, whereas remediation concerns rectifying something that is undesirable or deficient. Maintenance is proactive, remediation is reactive.

Some examples for non-functional upgrades are listed below:

- Updates to technology versions to provide or prolong vendor support, including the renewal or extension of licensing arrangements

- Provision of appropriate levels of resilience and disaster recovery

- Implementation of fixes and patches to address security vulnerabilities

- Migration to strategic technology platforms in order to realise the benefits of rationalisation and achieve sustainable cost savings, for example through the use of virtual environments rather than dedicated hardware

- Improvements to performance and/or capacity to accommodate
  future growth

- Refactoring of application code to improve maintainability with respect
  to both troubleshooting and functional improvements

Please note, although an attempt has been made here to list these examples in descending order of importance, this order is debatable and may vary from one organisation to another.

What Green Point Analysis Is And Is Not

In order to put to bed some early misconceptions let's describe what Green Point Analysis is and, perhaps more importantly, what it isn't.

Green Point Analysis is:
- A means of quantifying the value gained from maintenance and
  remediation activities undertaken to upgrade the middleware,
  infrastructure and the non-functional aspect of application software

- A methodology that provides a unit of measurement, a green point, to
  quantify the benefits achieved following computer system maintenance

- A method of comparison that reflects the relative importance of
  the work undertaken by the different information systems within an
  organisation's system estate

- Flexible and adaptable to suit both organisation and business domain

Green Point Analysis is not:
- A universal metric intended to be used across organisations or, indeed,
  in the wider information technology industry; however if Green Point
  Analysis and the weighting coefficients it uses are applied consistently
  it will provide a unit of measurement useful when considering
  maintenance activity within an organisation

- A fixed set of rules, but rather a methodology that can be adapted to
  align with the domain in which it applies and the related business and
  technical considerations of the organisation using it

What's In This Book?

The following provides a chapter by chapter summary of what can be found in the remainder of this book.

Chapter 2 - Background

A discussion of information system maintenance that describes how Green Point Analysis can be used to inform decisions and direct investment in maintenance activities more effectively. This chapter also describes the importance of transactions in Green Point Analysis and the application of weighting coefficients to acknowledge the business benefit delivered by different types of transaction.

Chapter 3 - Measuring Maintenance

The measurement of system maintenance work presents several challenges. This chapter describes some of the options available and concludes that there is a need for a metric that allows us to understand the value embedded by maintenance activities.

Chapter 4 - Green Point Analysis

An overview of Green Point Analysis, the method used to calculate green points and its key concepts. This chapter explains how a transaction is found at the core of a green point and how weighting coefficients are used to exaggerate or diminish the status of a transaction processed by a particular system to better reflect its value to the business.

Chapter 5 - Transactions

A detailed discussion of the transactions used as the basis of green point calculation. This chapter lists some of the potential candidates for transactions for use in Green Point Analysis and rounds off with a description of transaction class, in which the concepts of supported and recovered transactions are explained.

Chapter 6 - Weighting Coefficients

Weighting coefficients are multiplying factors applied to a transaction to exaggerate or diminish its relative importance. A green point is the product of applying one or more weighting coefficients to a transaction. This chapter lists some of the coefficients organisations may choose in their Green Point Analysis and provides some example values.

Chapter 7 - Maintenance Life/Technology Count

Maintenance life is the extended period of support delivered by maintenance and remediation activities. This chapter shows how support extension and capacity reduction are used in the determination of maintenance. In addition to this the concept of technology count is defined.

Chapter 8 - Green Point Calculation

A description of the equations used by Green Point Analysis to calculate green points. This chapter details the equations and provides a worked example of their use.

Chapter 9 - Applications of Green Point Analysis

A summary of some applications of Green Point Analysis. This chapter lists a number of potential uses of the method including prioritising of options, high-level estimating and ongoing audit and monitoring.

Chapter 10 - System Health

The discussion of the use of health lenses to evaluate system health. This chapter, which is somewhat of an aside to Green Point Analysis, presents an idea on how system health may be analysed and communicated using some of the same system characteristics considered when selecting weighting coefficients.

Chapter 11 - Conclusion

Where Can I Get Further Help?

If you would like clarification on any of the aspects of Green Point Analysis raised in this book or would like to discuss the implementation of Green Point Analysis in your organisation, please contact us via the website www.greenpts.org.

Chapter 2 - Background

We spend vast amounts implementing new information technology systems, but do we, does your organisation, spend enough ensuring this technology remains current and therefore robust and fit for purpose throughout the course of its working life?

In an ideal world, your system estate would be running on current hardware, with the most up-to-date operating systems and components (servers, content management systems, messaging technology and so on) patched to the most recent versions. It is perhaps more likely that you will be operating with budget constraints, focusing on delivering new functionality to expand and improve your business. The consequence of this is the budget available to keep your system estate current will be tight. If this is the case, then it is important to direct what resources you do have in the most efficient and effective manner.

Even if you are fortunate enough not to have significant budget constraints, you should still look to prioritise expenditure in a manner that best serves your business. If good use can be made of the funds set aside for maintenance, then it may be possible to make savings and release some of the budget for change projects that enhance the business proposition and generate more revenue. Perhaps more realistically, if the historical management of your information system has been a little lax, then it will be useful to have a method that helps you to prioritise the various initiatives you need to undertake in order to meet the most pressing needs first.

The problem with maintenance and remediation is that it is very difficult to write a business case for the associated investment. It is an investment in something you already have, which will not result in an increase in business benefit. Unlike change activity where you are investing to make something happen, such as the generation of some additional business revenue, with maintenance you are ensuring that something doesn't happen, i.e. a technology failure. It's a hard sell, especially if you are competing for budget with change initiatives claiming tangible business benefits. However, the costs will be very real in the event of a system failure that affects the ability to do business. A system outage will probably lead to the tangible impact of lost business as well as less quantifiable consequences, such as a loss of customer confidence and reputational damage.

When it comes to system maintenance, there is a level of the unknown. Old, out-of-date and unsupported software may still run quite happily without issue. As time passes it will likely develop vulnerabilities; however these may not be exposed and it is therefore possible that they will not manifest themselves as major issues.

If implementing new functionality and systems is an investment, then keeping the system estate you have built well-maintained and under supplier support can be analogised as insurance. Insurance is not arranged in the expectation that a claim will be made. Likewise, supplier support is not bought with either the vendor or the purchaser expecting there to be a regular dialogue between the two organisations. The support contract needs to be in place in order that it can be called upon when required.

Another analogy would be that of the purchase of a new car. If you go to the expense of buying a car, it is advisable to keep it serviced and maintained. This is particularly relevant if a failure to keep the vehicle serviced invalidates your warranty. There may well be similarities with the technology your organisation has purchased. It is common for vendors to only support the most recent versions of their product, due to the impracticalities and cost-efficiency of supporting a decreasing number of customers using older versions.

Once the importance of system maintenance is appreciated, the next question is how do we measure it? As you will see in the next chapter there are a few options. We can view maintenance from a cost perspective and the amount we have invested in the undertaking of it. Alternatively, we can take an earned value view and express maintenance in terms of amount of work, or work packages, completed. Finally, we can use a metric that considers the business value of the work undertaken.

The metric for maintenance proposed in this book is that of a green point. A green point is a measure of the value embedded by the maintenance and remediation activities. Until this concept is elaborated upon later, it is perhaps best to think of a green point as a square foot of maintenance. A green point is not a universal metric. It can be customised to better suit the organisation in which it is employed. Green points allow quantitative comparison of options and initiatives, along with a way of tracking the progress of maintenance activities over time. Green points are calculated using Green Point Analysis.

In this book, we will talk about claiming green points, i.e. if we progress Option A, it will result in x green points being claimed, whereas Option B will give us y points. Green points are claimed at the point the maintenance or remediation project is implemented. Consequently, we can audit how much effort we are investing in maintenance by keeping track of the green points claimed each year. When it comes to retrospective activities, such as audit and investment tracking, we talk in terms of delivered green points. Claiming and delivering green points is discussed in more detail later.

The name green point comes from two ideas. Firstly, we have 'green', a word normally associated with health, renewal and rebirth, and then we have 'points', a score or tally. Green points are conceptual and may, and probably should, differ from organisation to organisation. It could be that an assessment of the green points on similar activities in different companies will give widely differing results. What is important is that green points are calculated consistently across an initiative and, if ongoing metrics are being sought, across your organisation and the projects that Green Point Analysis is being used to assess.

It will make no sense to the outside world to say, "We updated our server farm and claimed 10,000 green points." It should, however, provide additional insight within your organisation if you can say, "Option A, in which we upgrade System X and System Y concurrently, allows us to claim 7,000 green points, whereas Option B, where we upgrade System X then System Y, results in a claim of 8,500 green points."

Similarly, if you apply Green Point Analysis consistently, it allows an assessment over time. If you claimed 100,000 green points last year and incurred ten days of downtime, as opposed to claiming 50,000 green points the previous year and seeing twenty days of outage, it is easy to draw a correlation between effort expended on maintenance and system stability. It's not quite that simple because green points 'claimed' in one year may be 'delivered' in another. Again, more of this later.

This is not to say green points cannot be made more tangible. If you know how many green points each maintenance initiative claims and what will be spent or, even better, has been spent, it's a simple calculation to determine the cost of claiming a green point. If this is tracked, over time you will be able to understand how effective you are at delivering maintenance initiatives. You can also use green point cost to gauge benefits you have gained from improvements in the way you work.

So, what is Green Point Analysis? Green Point Analysis is anchored to the premise that the level of activity a system is supporting is a key consideration when we are prioritising and directing maintenance effort. It looks at the number of transactions processed by a system and then applies a number of weighting coefficients to exaggerate or diminish the status of a transaction processed by a particular system to better reflect its business importance. A green point is essentially a transaction, or perhaps group of transactions, that has been manipulated by one or more weighting coefficients to reflect its relative value. Put simply, it is a transaction that has been made to look bigger or smaller. If it weren't for weighting coefficients, Green Point Analysis would lead to you claiming one green point for each transaction running in support. Following the application of some weighting coefficients, each transaction might claim 0.8 or 1.2 green points. The equations shown later may look complicated, however the concept is reasonably simple.

Weighting coefficients are important in Green Point Analysis as they allow us to factor in the relative importance of the work done across an organisation's system estate. We would all prefer our systems to be running at their optimum and most robust; however the practicalities are that some things will not be. Resource and budget constraints will require maintenance work to be prioritised.

Weighting coefficients provide a way of combining competing considerations to allow a numeric comparison of their relative importance. These considerations will include competing views from different areas of a business. For example, more business-minded stakeholders will be interested in ensuring systems are well-maintained and revenue streams are protected, whereas those tasked with managing and maintaining will also be keen to ensure system rationalisation in accordance with the organisation's system architecture strategy, in order to make the estate easier to maintain and more cost-effective to run.

Please note, you can't claim green points by doing nothing. A green point is only claimed when maintenance leads to a future transaction being supported (processed by a supported technology) or being recovered (not lost due to an outage). Green Point Analysis will help you understand the value in taking a particular course of action. If we do this, we will get x, if we do that, we will get y, with x and y measured in green points.

Chapter 3 - Measuring Maintenance

"Nowadays people know the price of everything and the value of nothing."
Oscar Wilde

Is this observation by Oscar Wilde, who died in 1900, any less relevant today? Investment in information systems can be a costly affair, especially if you consider the whole life of the system and the maintenance cost over the course of its life. If you are going to incur these costs, it's better to incur them wisely.

In order to make wise decisions you need to be aware of the pertinent facts. When it comes to managing projects, a key factor will be the amount of work that is being undertaken. In addition to this it is useful to understand the value or benefit in carrying out this work.

In this chapter we discuss the options available to track system maintenance projects and propose a metric that considers the value embedded by the maintenance of information systems.

Measuring the Cost

Perhaps the simplest way to measure maintenance is by the amount of money you spend in undertaking it. Assuming an appropriate level of diligence is applied, it is likely that there will be a correlation between the amount invested and the service levels delivered.

Given that maintenance is perpetual in nature, and will probably not have a natural end point, other than when the system is decommissioned, it makes some sense to allocate a specific budget for maintenance activities. The pitfall here is to assume that not spending the budget means you haven't met your targets. The budget should be the sum of the estimated costs of the work you intend to do. As with all things, savings can be made. The focus should therefore be on completing the work you set out to do, and not on spending the budget. There is always the option of undertaking more maintenance than you originally intended; however this may put you into the realms of diminishing returns. It may be better to bank any savings.

When it comes to budgets, people sometimes talk in terms of burn rate, the inference being that if you are spending at a rate that indicates you will use up the budget by the end of the period it covers, all is good. This seems counter-intuitive. The point of a project is to deliver the benefits of the business case, not to spend the budget. Delivering the project at a discount, with some money to return to the business, is a good not a bad thing. A fixation on burn rate is a particular bugbear of ours, as this is analogous to measuring the progress of the Titanic in bags of coal.

Given the nature of maintenance, there may be opportunities to make savings.

If maintenance work is rolled into change activities occurring around the same time, the resulting rationalisation should serve to reduce costs. It makes little sense implementing a new application on out-of-date infrastructure. You may also find that those more accustomed to estimating for change activity overestimate the effort involved in maintenance work. The level of uncertainty for maintenance work will generally be less than for change activity introducing new functionality, therefore allowances for estimating tolerance and contingency should not need to be as high. For these reasons maintenance work is more likely to come in under budget than over. If this is the case, then it is incorrect to see an underspend on the budget as a missed objective.

The setting of budgets can also drive undesirable behaviour. In some organisations, if a budget is underutilised one year then the budget for the following year will be reduced. This doesn't make a great deal of sense. The budget should relate to the work you plan to do, not what you have or haven't done previously. Driving the work with the budget is a case of the tail wagging the dog. There is no simple answer to this; however it may be worth looking at how your budgets are agreed.

Bringing in a project under budget has to be a good thing. This is as true for system maintenance as it is any other type of work. Spending money in order to achieve a burn rate and use up all the budget is difficult to justify. The amount spent on an initiative can be achieved by delivering more than that defined in the original brief, i.e. gold-plating. From a project perspective, gold-plating is arguably worse than scope creep. Scope creep due to the introduction of new requirements should result in improvements to the product. Gold-plating is likely to involve the undertaking of work that is outside the remit of both the original scope and any subsequent variations requested by or on behalf of the sponsor.

Measuring the Value

Given the problems associated with measuring maintenance in terms of cost, it seems better not to view maintenance in terms of what you are spending on it, but rather by what is actually delivered. A project management technique called earned value management exists to do this.

Earned value management measures project performance and progress in an objective manner. Typically, earned value management involves dividing the tasks included in a project into units of work or work packages. The value of each work package is then expressed, or rather estimated, as a cost. The delivery of the work packages is then distributed across the duration of the project to show when the 'planned value' is expected to be delivered. Once the project progresses and the work packages are completed, this is tracked as 'earned value', which may be ahead of or after what was originally planned. In addition to this, earned value management also tracks the 'actual cost' of delivering the work. In doing so, unlike burn rate, it decouples the value of what is being delivered from the cost incurred in achieving this.

Earned value management is useful in that it encourages a focus on the value you have achieved, rather than the cost of the work. It will serve to highlight instances where although you may not be spending the entire budget, you are still completing the work you intended to. Actual cost is still there and this is the same thing as burn rate, but you also have earned value expressed by estimated cost of a delivered work package. For example, this would allow you to demonstrate that you had delivered £10,000 worth of maintenance at the cost of just £8,000, and thus present a positive message to interested stakeholders.

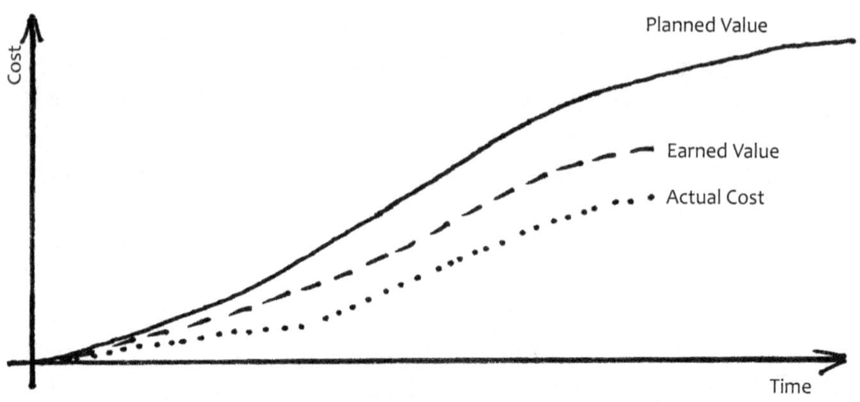

Earned Value Management

The graph above shows a positive cost variance. The actual cost is trending below the earned value so all is good as the project is tracking under budget. This would be good if it were not for the negative schedule variance demonstrated by the earned value sitting below the planned value. Therefore, in this scenario the project manager needs to find ways to speed things up a little in order to bring the delivery of earned value more in line with the plan, ideally without adversely impacting the cost variance.

Although earned value management provides a good understanding of the value you are delivering (earning) against the costs you are incurring, it does not provide any indication of the business value gained from undertaking this work. This is not a criticism as earned value management is not meant to do this. The assumption is that the benefit of delivering the work was considered at its conception.

To better understand the benefit delivered by the maintenance of systems, we need to look inside the box or boxes and understand what the components we are upgrading are doing, i.e. it's more about the work the system is doing than the work being done to maintain it.

A Maintenance Metric

This book proposes a metric that evaluates the value embedded by the maintenance of information systems. That is to say it considers the work the systems are doing and the business benefit of this work. Whereas earned value management refers to the work done to the system, this metric evaluates the maintenance work done by the system. The unit of this metric is a green point.

Green Point Analysis looks inside the boxes at the work the systems are doing and considers the benefit of this work from both business and technical perspectives. As you will see later, green points are calculated using Green Point Analysis, a method that, to some extent, is comparable to Function Point Analysis (FPA).

FPA is a technique used in software development to determine, or rather estimate, how much business functionality is being delivered. In FPA a unit of measure called a function point is used to express the size of the system. The number of function points is calculated by examining aspects of the system such as outputs, inquiries, inputs, internal files and external interfaces. Think of it as a way to determine how many square feet of software development will be delivered. At the risk of oversimplifying this much-criticised technique, which fails to recognise the complexity of the logic required to deliver this functionality, function points are essentially channels of system interactions, by either a user or system interface.

Whereas function points provide a metric for sizing software, green points provide a metric for expressing the value embedded by maintaining it. Green points allow us to determine how much maintenance we are delivering. This time let's think of them as square feet of system maintenance. In the case of green points, however, the analogy breaks down. Green points are conceptual in nature and variable in size.

The assertion that runs through the remainder of this book is that it is not the number of channels or the complexity of a system that is relevant to maintenance, but the number of times these channels are being hit. As you will see, at the core of a green point is a transaction. If all things were equal, the maintenance of a system supporting twice the transactions of another would claim twice as many green points. Green Point Analysis recognises that this may not be the case and that different transactions may have different value to your organisation.

It is important to remember that green points do not provide a universal metric. It is a unit of comparison that allows us to assess the relative benefit of maintaining the systems across a technology estate with a view to the prioritisation work, such as the non-functional upgrades listed in the introduction. In addition to this, green points can be used as an audit measure to track the effectiveness of maintenance activities with time.

In the interests of transparency, it should be noted that Green Point Analysis steals concepts from both earned value management and FPA. From earned value management it borrows the understanding that the cost of doing work and the value realised by completing it are separate and can be uncoupled, and from FPA it takes the idea of using a conceptual metric. In FPA this metric is used to determine how much work there is to do. In Green Point Analysis the metric is a measure of the value gained from doing the work.

Chapter 4 - Green Point Analysis

Green Point Analysis provides a method of quantifying the value gained from maintenance and remediation activities undertaken to upgrade the middleware, infrastructure and the non-functional aspect of application software. This value is expressed as a metric called a green point.

Green points provide a scoring mechanism useful in the prioritisation of options across a project or portfolio of projects. They can also be used to track the effectiveness of system maintenance activities over time.

This chapter describes the key concepts of Green Point Analysis, the method used to calculate green points.

Transactions

At the core of a green point is a transaction of some type. As you will see later in this book, not all transactions are considered equal; however their prevalence is always worthy of consideration. In its crudest form a green point can be claimed when a maintenance activity leads to a future transaction running on infrastructure with an appropriate level of maintenance. An appropriate level of maintenance is deemed as one where elements such as current technology versions and vendor support need to be in place.

Green Point Analysis classifies transactions into one of two types: supported transactions and recovered transactions. A supported transaction is a transaction that as a result of system maintenance will run on supported technology. A recovered transaction is a transaction that will run on supported technology, which would have been lost due to an outage if it were not for system maintenance.

When it comes to transactions we talk about transaction rates, i.e. the number occurring over a particular period. If we know the period of time that system maintenance is extending the support by, we can calculate the number of transactions we are impacting. Within Green Point Analysis, this period is called the maintenance life and is discussed later in this chapter.

Note that if the number of transactions a system processes is uncertain or unknown then a relative estimating technique known as T-shirt sizing can be used. An example of this is included in the appendices.

Weighting Coefficients

Green Point Analysis recognises that the work done by some systems will be of greater benefit to the business than that undertaken by others. This is reflected by the use of weighting coefficients. A green point is the result of applying one or more weighting coefficients to a transaction. Weighting coefficients are used in the calculation of green points to exaggerate or diminish the relative importance of a transaction to the business.

Weighting coefficients are used to combine competing considerations. These will include the viewpoints of both those responsible for running your business and those tasked with ensuring the supporting technology is robust and cost-effective. Generally, a number of weighting coefficients will be used in green point calculation. These may be applied to the supported transactions, the recovered transactions or both.

Maintenance Life

The maintenance life is the period over which green points can be claimed, i.e. used in comparisons and prioritisations. It is the extension to the support period provided by system maintenance and remediation activities.

In the case of remediation, where the system is no longer supported, the maintenance life starts when the maintenance upgrades are implemented. Alternatively, the maintenance life starts when the previous period of support ends. Green Point Analysis focuses on the beneficial impacts of maintenance. Therefore, it does not concern the length of the support period but rather the extent to which it is extended.

Generally, the maintenance life ends at the end of the support period. The exception to this is when a system reaches and exceeds its capacity before the end of the support period. In these circumstances the maintenance life is taken to end at this point. The assumption here is that a system's ability to process transactions is compromised when it is working above its capacity.

Technology Count

Finally, we have technology count. If maintenance activity leads to upgrades of more than one technology, then it makes sense to reflect this in the calculation of green points. The calculation is simple. If you upgrade two technologies, you can claim twice as many green points and so on. Please note, it may be that the maintenance lives of the technologies may not align. In this case a conservative approach can be taken, where the shortest maintenance life is used or the technologies can be assessed in isolation, with the green points of each assessment being tallied to give a total.

The following diagram pulls together the concepts discussed in this chapter and presents them in the format that you will see throughout this book. In this diagram the x-axis represents time, the y-axis shows transaction rate and the z-axis, going into the page, illustrates the technology count. As you will see in similar diagrams in this book, green points are represented as a shaded area, with those due to supported and recovered transactions shown above and below the x-axis respectively.

Also note the annotation along the x-axis. In these diagrams the origin of the graph, where the axes cross, represents the point at which the maintenance upgrade is implemented. In the scenario shown here, green points are not claimed until the point in time where the previous support period ended. In addition to this, green points are not claimed for the full extent of the support period. This is due to capacity being reached ahead of this point.

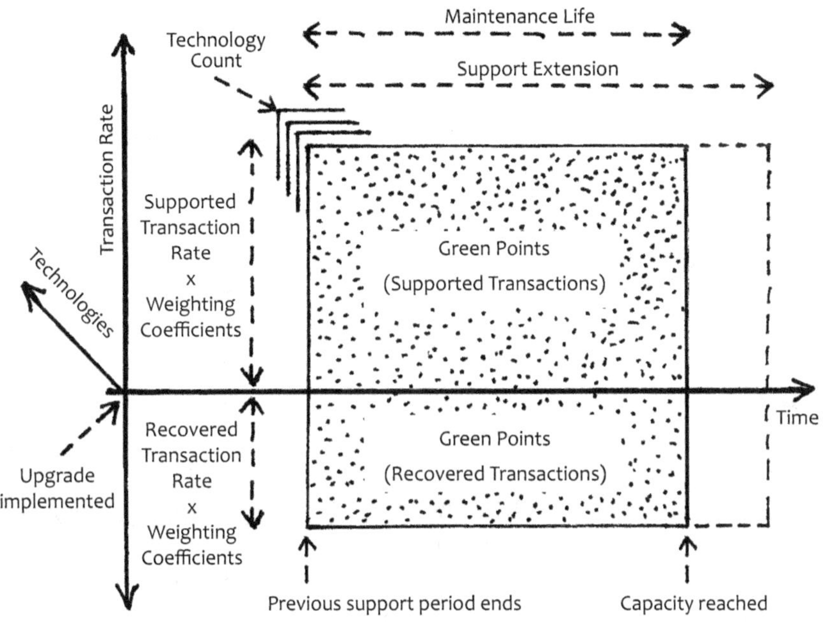

Green Point Analysis Concepts

Please note, if you are comfortable with the concepts shown here, perhaps as a result of a training course, you may wish to skip the following three chapters and jump straight to Chapter 8 - Green Point Calculation.

Chapter 5 - Transactions

The calculation of green points starts with the number of transactions a system is expected to process. Depending on the type of information systems you are maintaining, transactions can take several different forms. Within the context of Green Point Analysis, a transaction is taken to be a processing event, i.e. an item of work performed by the system. This processing event may be triggered by a user interaction; it may be system generated or it could involve a combination of both.

This chapter lists some of the potential candidates for transactions for use in Green Point Analysis and rounds off with a description of transaction class, in which the concepts of supported and recovered transactions are explained.

Transaction Candidates

Given how central transactions are to Green Point Analysis, it is important to consider which ones are best to use in green point calculation. Depending on the type of organisation you work in, there may be several possibilities as to the transactions you choose to use. This decision should consider what is most important to your organisation. A list of candidates for transactions follows:

Page Impressions

Perhaps the simplest transaction to consider is that of a page impression, a straightforward read-only display of a web page. In this situation, each instance of a web server serving up a page to a website visitor is taken to be a transaction.

Page impressions will be useful transaction types when you are managing several web offerings. A good example here might be where a company is hosting several stand-alone internet presences and needs to perform an upgrade or patch. An understanding of which website is serving up the most pages is useful information to have when it comes to planning your upgrades.

Please note, when considering websites and the number of page impressions, there could be a temptation to think in terms of unique visitors. The number of unique visitors may be a useful statistic elsewhere; however with respect to maintaining systems, ten people making one visit is not a great deal different to one person hitting the servers ten times. It could be argued that the number of unique visitors is a relevant consideration, as the outage of a system with a lot of uniques will impact more people, but then it could be said that one loyal and regular patron is as valuable as ten more casual ones.

If you think the unique visitor count serves your purpose better than the number of page impressions, then there is no issue with using this. Green Point Analysis is perfectly valid whatever you choose to use as a transaction.

System Interactions

Another potential candidate for use as a transaction is a system interaction. Given that the page impression discussed previously is a system interaction, it's wise to define what we mean by this. If we view a page impression as a read-only transaction, then a system interaction is an activity leading to some information being written, i.e. it is an interaction where stored data is created, updated or deleted.

Given the nature of information systems, especially public-facing ones, it may well be that the proposition supported by the system integrates both brochureware or read-only content, and functionality to support interaction with the system users. Examples of this would include a blog, a social networking site, or a system supporting some sort of financial transaction. More on these later. In the case of a system where you have various transaction types to pick from, you will need to decide which are worthiest of consideration. The expectation is that when faced with a choice between a read and a write interaction, it is the latter that is the more likely candidate to be used as the transaction in Green Point Analysis. This is not to say that the read-only/content-providing aspect of the system is not important, it is just not being used in the comparison of options.

You may be faced with a scenario where you are considering two systems so different in nature that the candidate transactions available on one system do not feature on the other. If this is the case, you need to find a way of accommodating what you do have, to reflect the relative importance to the business of the transactions you have available. This is discussed in more detail later under the heading Multi-Type Transactions.

As mentioned at the beginning of this chapter, there may also be system interactions which are not directly triggered by a system user. An example of this would be a batch job which when run would result in a number of system interactions or transactions being generated. In Green Point Analysis the way in which a transaction is triggered should not, and probably will not, make any appreciable difference. A transaction is a transaction, regardless of how it comes to be.

Retail Transactions

A retail transaction is essentially a specialist system interaction involving a financial consideration. If your role includes the management and/or maintenance of e-commerce systems, such as those used by online retailers, you will probably appreciate the importance of not losing any sales. Consequently, system interactions involving the sale of a product are strong candidates for use in Green Point Analysis.

Banking Transactions

As with the retail transactions referred to previously, a banking transaction can be seen as a specialist type of system interaction. In a large bank providing a range of financial services, the types of transactions will be numerous. Examples include deposits and withdrawals on banking accounts, the generation of statements, and updates to share and fund unit prices.

As previously discussed these transactions will be triggered by users, the systems themselves, and possibly interbank transfers generated by the systems of external organisations.

Multi-Type Transactions

One of the beauties of Green Point Analysis is its simplicity. It is not intended to be an exact science. Consequently there is very little point in layering on additional complexity. When it comes to selecting what type of transaction you will use in your green point calculation, it is easier to select the same or a similar candidate, but if this is not possible then all is not lost.

Faced with a scenario where your analysis needs include consideration of disparate transaction types, an assessment should be made of the relative importance of these transactions. It may be that the transactions involving a system interaction with a financial aspect are considered ten times more important than read-only page impressions delivering content. If this is the case, you either multiply the former by ten or divide the latter by the same amount.

Perhaps a better way to explain this is with the application of a coefficient. The use of coefficients is key to Green Point Analysis and is discussed in more detail later. It doesn't make much difference how you approach this, but the use of a coefficient does make it a little clearer. If, in the above example, we use a Normalisation Coefficient (C_N) and let it take the value of 10.0 in the case of system interactions and 1.0 for page impressions, then this can serve to reduce any confusion if the number of transactions is ever questioned, i.e. we can keep things separate and show the workings out.

Software Tools

As you work with green points you will hopefully begin to appreciate how widely they can be applied. There are, however, systems where there is no obvious candidate for a transaction. An example of this would be the applications used to support a system, such as those involved in system design, development and implementation. Although these systems are indirectly involved in maintaining the effective operation of a business it is still important that they are kept current and up to date. Other examples would include word processors, spreadsheets and perhaps even internet browsers. For scenarios such as these the model could be adapted to use the time the system is used, i.e. a transaction could be taken as a work hour.

Transaction Class

A primary driver for maintaining systems is to ensure the transactions processed by these systems are processed successfully on supported technologies. Consequently, Green Point Analysis classifies transactions into one of two types.

Supported Transactions

First, we have those transactions which, as a result of system maintenance, will run on supported technology. When maintenance activity extends the time for which a system is in support, then supported transactions are taken to be the transactions occurring in that period.

Reliance on unsupported technology is undesirable from the perspective of the business underpinned by those systems and those responsible for ensuring their availability. Essentially, the use of unsupported technology presents a risk. Out-of-date versions of technology will have a greater propensity for failure, and therefore outages, and the time taken to recover from outages, in the absence of full support, will likely be greater. In Green Point Analysis, the removal of risks such as these is assumed to be value-adding.

Recovered Transactions

Perhaps more prevalent are those transactions that are currently not being processed due to system outages. The assumption here is that, in the absence of intervention, this situation will persist. It may be that workarounds have been put in place to mitigate these outages; however these could require manual intervention and consequently carry a risk of failing. Either way, the situation is not ideal. System outages impair the ability to do business and can damage reputation and brand.

Green Point Analysis recognises the value of reducing or eradicating system outages. Where the maintenance of a system results in fewer system outages and a consequential increase in the number of transactions processed then these transactions are referred to as recovered transactions. For those who prefer a graphical view, the following diagram provides a representation of supported and recovered transactions. In this chart the shaded area above the x-axis (time) represents the number of supported transactions resulting from the maintenance activity, with the number of recovered transactions shown below.

In this slightly simplified view, we can see how the number of each class of transaction can be taken as the rate at which they occur over the period for which we are allowed to claim an improvement. This period, known as the maintenance life, is taken to be the period between the point at which the previous period of support expires to the point at which the support extension delivered by maintenance work ends.

Note, the maintenance life may be taken to end before the support expiry when the system exceeds its processing capacity. This is discussed in more detail in Chapter 7.

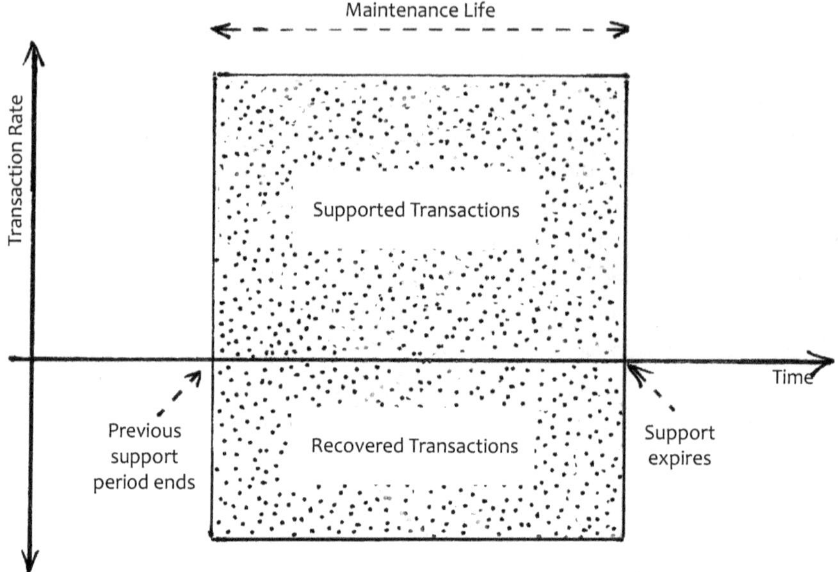

Supported and Recovered Transactions

Chapter 6 - Weighting Coefficients

The previous chapter discussed the candidate transactions for use in green point calculation. Although the number of transactions processed by a system is a key consideration in Green Point Analysis, the method also considers the relative importance of transactions. The number of transactions is an important factor when it comes to analysing the value in undertaking maintenance work; however, it is also useful to consider the relative importance of transactions to the business.

That is to say it is unlikely that all transactions are equal and some may take priority over others. It is therefore unsafe to compare systems purely in terms of number of transactions. Indeed, it is also unsound to view supported and recovered transactions with equal importance. It is probable that the recovery of transactions lost due to system outages will be more of a concern than bringing transactions running on unsupported technologies into support. A lost transaction is an immediate issue, whereas an unsupported transaction is more like a risk that has the potential to manifest itself as an issue.

In order to accommodate all things not being equal, Green Point Analysis makes use of weighting coefficients to exaggerate or diminish the value of a transaction to give a better reflection of its importance. A green point is the product of applying one or more weighting coefficients to a transaction. This chapter lists some of the coefficients organisations may choose in their Green Point Analysis and provides some example values.

Weighting Coefficients

Weighting coefficients provide a way of finessing green points to recognise that not all transactions processed by an organisation's system estate will be of the same priority. They provide a way of combining competing factors to allow a numeric comparison of their relative importance.

As you will see below, weighting coefficients can be used to reflect both the interests of the core business of your organisation and those concerned with maintaining a rationalised and robust system estate. What we are saying is there are two strategies at play here: that of the business and how it intends to both preserve and grow revenue, and that of information technologists tasked with managing and maintaining the organisation's estate of systems. Different stakeholders will view systems through different lenses and will have different priorities. Weighting coefficients provide a way of amalgamating these priorities.

It should be noted that the list of weighting coefficients used will and should vary from organisation to organisation. What is important in one business domain may not be applicable to another. Similarly, the range of values each coefficient may take should vary to suit both the organisation and domain which the systems support.

The six key weighting coefficients listed below are not mandatory to green point calculations and can be selected and rejected as appropriate to your business organisation. Indeed, the coefficients listed in this book and the range of values they take are mentioned primarily for the purpose of providing examples. Some other weighting coefficients are listed in the appendices.

Tiering Coefficient

In some organisations, particularly those subject to external regulation, certain systems will be more crucial to the core operation of the business than others. In the example of a bank, those systems required to support core banking activity will be deemed by regulators to be more important than a sales platform. In such scenarios, it is useful to tier your systems to reflect their importance. The classification of systems in this way allows rules to be set with respect to minimum service levels. In addition to this, tiering can also be used to prioritise maintenance effort; as such it is an excellent candidate for use as a weighting coefficient.

The labelling of tiers may well differ between organisations and industry; however within this book we use a tiering from 0 to 3 with Tier 0 being the most important. Consequently, the value of the tiering coefficient for a Tier 0 service will be much higher than that used for a Tier 3. As with all the weighting coefficients this has the effect of scaling the number of green points to reflect the importance of the service.

The tiering of systems also provides a good example of when Green Point Analysis could be disregarded. It could well be that you perform your analysis and the maintenance of a Tier 1 service would allow you to claim more green points that that of a Tier 0. If you considered green points in isolation you would prioritise the maintenance of the Tier 1 service; however business strategy, or even regulatory standards, may override your analysis and compel you to maintain the Tier 0 service first.

The following diagram provides a representation of how the tiering coefficient impacts the number of green points that can be claimed following maintenance activities. In this diagram the shaded area represents the number of green points claimed for the maintenance of a Tier 1 service. As you can see, if the service being maintained was a Tier 0 service then the shaded area would increase, i.e. the number of green points claimed would be more. Conversely, if efforts were directed towards maintaining a Tier 2 or 3 service then the number of green points claimed would reduce.

Note how the tiering coefficient is applied to both supported and recovered transactions.

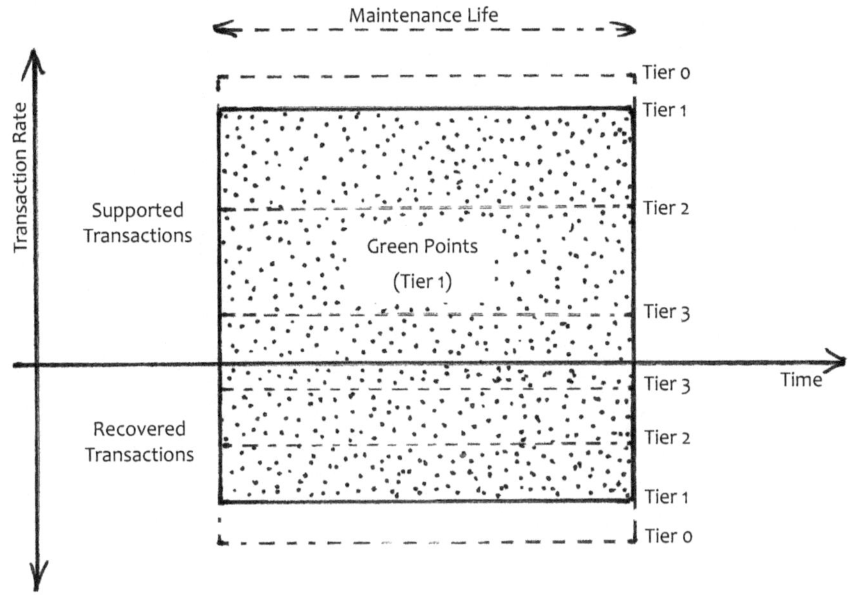

Green Points (Weighted by Tier)

Refactoring Coefficient

The refactoring coefficient recognises that tidy, maintainable application code is relevant to the number of transactions it processes. It seems reasonably safe to assume that there is more value in refactoring code that gets well-trafficked than that which is rarely used. The amount of refactoring required is also worthy of consideration. This coefficient therefore varies depending on the amount of refactoring effort required and, as with the tiering coefficient, scales the number of green points that can be claimed accordingly.

Please note, this coefficient relates to software running in the application layer of the system architecture. These applications may be bespoke applications developed in-house or proprietary software supplied by a vendor. The value the refactoring coefficient takes should reflect the amount of refactoring that will take place, the hope being this correlates to an improvement in code quality and reduction in technical debt. In the examples in this book we refer to refactoring using terms such as minor and major. This works quite well for proprietary software, in that the software version should serve as an indicator. For example, replacing version 3.2.1 of an application with version 3.2.2 would be seen as a minor, whereas a move from 3.2.1 to 3.3.0 would be deemed a major update. If we were to move from 3.2.1 to 4.0.0, we could then use the refactoring coefficient for a very major improvement. At the other end of the scale, a fix for a single defect would be taken to be very minor.

There is a case for removing this coefficient and including the application software in the technology count, i.e. the value reflecting the number of technologies being maintained. This is compelling if you consider that the upgrade to a new technology version should involve the introduction of a product that has had its underlying code refined and refactored since the previous edition. At least that is what you would hope. What we are therefore saying is that there is little logical difference between application software and lower-level middleware products, other than their respective positions in the software stack.

Architecture Coefficient

The architecture coefficient recognises that it makes good sense for an organisation to have a strategic architecture and, if it does, for its systems to align with it. This being the case, an organisation can rationalise its system estate and thus make it easier to maintain and more cost-effective to run. Consequently, if maintenance activity migrates a system to the strategic architecture, then this should be reflected in the number of green points claimed.

Please note, you can't claim green points by doing nothing. If a system running on the strategic architecture remains on that architecture then nothing from an architectural perspective has changed and no value has been embedded. Green points are a metric for added value.

There is also a scenario where you might choose to move away from the strategic architecture. There could be a particular opportunity that your business wants to exploit and the best way to do this is to buy in some proprietary kit that sits outside your strategy. In this case the number of green points that can be claimed will be reduced.

There is an argument to say there are varying grades of architectural compliance; however in the examples shown in this book you are either compliant or you are not. That is not to say it is not appropriate for your organisation to take a different approach. If an existing process for grading architectural compliance exists, this can be incorporated into Green Point Analysis.

Strategy Coefficient

As businesses evolve and grow, their long-term strategies will be revised and adapted. One of the consequences of this is that systems implemented to support your business strategy historically may not align quite so well with your current plans. Therefore, if you're faced with the choice of maintaining several systems, some of which support the current business strategy and some that don't, then it is useful to include this consideration in your Green Point Analysis.

When it comes to business strategy, things are perhaps not as clear-cut as they were for the architectural strategy discussed previously. It may well be that systems support the business's drive to exploit a particular opportunity to varying degrees. For example, if a business is looking to drive sales then sales systems will be key to this strategy; however this is not to say that those systems that service the ongoing support resulting from these sales are not contributing to some extent. In the examples shown in this book, the strategy coefficient can take a range of values depending on how well the service supplied by a system aligns with the business strategy.

Security Coefficient

Whether you're interested in preserving and growing business revenue, or managing and maintaining the organisation's computer systems, information security vulnerabilities will be a concern. Ideally security vulnerabilities would be fixed as and when they are identified; however this may not always be possible. As with any change it is prudent to apply fixes in a controlled manner, with an appropriate level of testing and the proper adherence to implementation procedures. Therefore, there is a case to include security fixes with the release of other upgrades.

Given the importance of information security, in terms of both business revenue and reputation, if fixes are included in maintenance releases, then these implementations should score well in terms of green points. In the examples given in this book, the values used by the security coefficient are graded with the severity of the vulnerability, the most critical vulnerabilities serving to significantly increase the amount of green points that can be claimed by an initiative.

Outage Coefficient

Last, but definitely not least, we have the outage coefficient. This recognises the criticality of a lost transaction by greatly exaggerating the number of green points claimed for recovering one. In the examples shown here, a recovered transaction claims one hundred times more green points than a supported one. However, the value taken by this coefficient should be considered by each organisation utilising Green Point Analysis.

Weighting Coefficient Values

The following coefficient values are provided for use in the worked examples and case studies included in this book. This is not to say they are not useful in your implementation of Green Point Analysis, but rather they should only be used following due consideration. It may well be that it makes sense for your organisation to use a different set of weighting coefficients, or at least vary the range of coefficient values to accentuate the importance of a particular consideration to your business priorities. Examples of some other weighting coefficients are included in the appendices.

When it comes to deciding on the weighting coefficients, and the range of values they can take, it is useful to pick a few projects, plug in the numbers and see what prioritisation leads you to. If this is wildly out of kilter with what you might expect then you will need to adjust your use of Green Point Analysis to something which aligns with what your organisation regards as important.

If you take this proof of concept approach, then it will also be useful to poll the opinion of other stakeholders who have a vested interest in a well-managed system estate. The more diverse the people you choose to involve in this the better, as different viewpoints, viewed through different lenses, will serve to test the approach you are proposing. Indeed, you may uncover an aspect of business or system operation that leads you to include a new weighting coefficient. At the very least you may be compelled to consider adjusting the range of values a coefficient can take, as people with different perspectives will have different views as to what is and what isn't important.

The selection of weighting coefficients and the range of values they can take is not something that will be set in concrete. It is expected that your use of Green Point Analysis will be amended and refined over time. Given that Green Point Analysis is often used in comparative assessments, it is important to apply it consistently, i.e. the approach you adopt must be the same across the initiatives you are comparing. Basically, you need to compare like with like.

Consequently, if you are using Green Point Analysis to gather ongoing metrics to assess the effectiveness of your maintenance initiatives over time, you will need to settle on the weighting coefficients you are using. For example, you may choose to track the cost of claiming a green point for each project you deliver, thus building up a historical record of your maintenance activity. This would be a useful tool in assessing the effectiveness of any process improvement initiatives you are pursuing. The point here is if you adjust your use of weighting coefficients, then your new approach needs to be applied retrospectively to the historical data you hold.

The collection of historical data relating to your use of Green Point Analysis will be useful information. Once you have built up a decent sample, size you can experiment with the coefficient values you have been applying to see how they impact historical prioritisation. This sensitivity analysis could reveal insight that you can use to refine your weighting coefficient values going forward. It may well be that there is a particular weighting coefficient that isn't impacting on the results you are seeing and can therefore be discarded.

The weighting coefficients used in examples and case studies included in this book are shown below along with the values they may take.

Coefficient	Suggested Values
Tiering Coefficient (C_T)	Tier 0 = 1.0 Tier 1 = 0.8 Tier 2 = 0.5 Tier 3 = 0.2
Refactoring Coefficient (C_R)	None = 1.0 Very minor = 1.05 Minor = 1.1 Major = 1.2 Very major = 1.4
Architecture Coefficient (C_A)	System will move away from strategic architecture = 0.5 System stays on non-strategic architecture = 0.9 System uses strategic architecture = 1.0 System will move to strategic architecture = 1.2
Strategy Coefficient (C_S)	No alignment with business strategy = 1.0 Weak alignment with business strategy = 1.05 Reasonable alignment with business strategy = 1.1 Strong alignment with business strategy = 1.25 Very strong alignment with business strategy = 1.5
Security Coefficient (C_C)	No fixes implemented = 1.0 Very minor fixes implemented = 1.1 Minor fixes implemented = 1.3 Major fixes implemented = 1.6 Very major fixes implemented = 2.0
Outage Coefficient (C_O)	Resilience/disaster recovery within agreed limits = 1 Resilience/disaster recovery outside agreed limits = 100

Chapter 7 - Maintenance Life/Technology Count

In order to calculate the number of green points that can be claimed by a particular maintenance initiative, the period over which this calculation is performed must be determined. Within Green Point Analysis this period is termed the maintenance life. In addition to this the calculation of green points considers the number of technologies being maintained. This is reflected in green point calculation by a technology count.

This chapter describes both maintenance life and technology count within the context of Green Point Analysis.

Maintenance Life

Maintenance life is the additional time period of support that system maintenance provides. It is the period over which the system will operate under support and within capacity as a result of system maintenance. With respect to green point calculation, maintenance life is the period over which green points can be claimed, i.e. included in comparison and prioritisation exercises.

As you will see when we discuss support extension below, the maintenance life cannot start before the previous support period ends. Green Point Analysis calculates the value embedded by maintenance activities, therefore maintaining something that is already under support will score no points until the previous arrangement has expired.

Support Extension

The determination of maintenance life starts with support extension. This is the additional period of time that the system will be under support as a result of system maintenance. This may sound similar to the description given of maintenance life given previously, however the crucial difference is the absence of the mention of system capacity.

The start of this period is determined in one of two ways. If the system in question is out of support and therefore requires remediation, the support extension starts at the point the maintenance upgrade is implemented and the system is brought back into support.

If the system is to be upgraded before the current period of support expires, then it is being maintained rather than remediated. In this case we are extending the support, therefore existing support arrangements must be considered. Consequently, the support extension starts from the point the current support ends.

The following diagrams show from a green points perspective what remediation and maintenance projects might look like respectively. In the first diagram the green points are claimed from the point at which the upgrade is implemented, i.e.

where the axes cross. In the second case, where the existing support arrangements do not end until a period after the upgrade is implemented, the claiming of green points is delayed.

In both situations, we are sticking with the assumption that the system will not experience capacity issues within the period of the support extension. Consequently, support extension and maintenance life end at the same time and are equal. Technology count is discussed later.

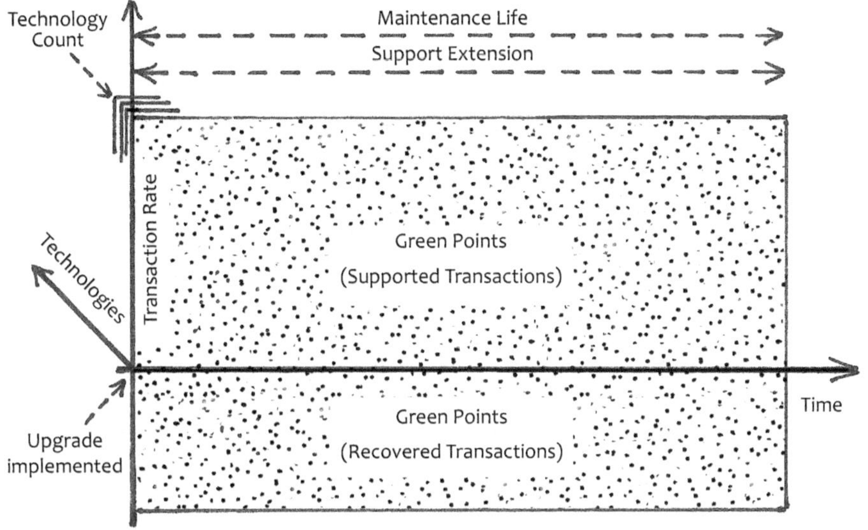

Support Extension (Remediation)

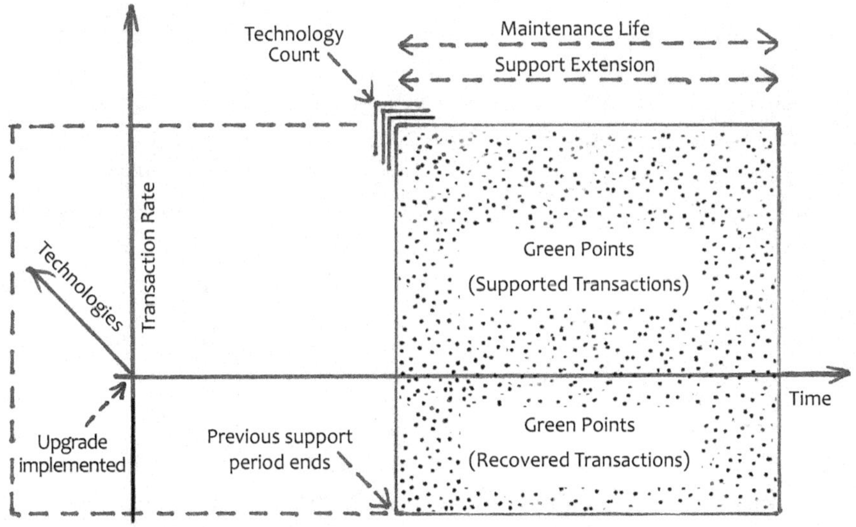

Support Extension (Maintenance)

Capacity Reduction

Capacity reduction accommodates situations where the capacity of the system is reached before the end of the support extension. It assumes the ability of the system to process transactions is compromised once it exceeds its capacity. Given the greater propensity for outages of systems running above their design capacity, the service level achieved is likely to be questionable. In addition to this, the service agreement may only be valid if the system is working within agreed operational limits. For these reasons, transactions processed by systems running above their design capacity are disregarded. This has the effect of shortening the maintenance life and, consequently, the period over which green points can be claimed.

To disregard the transactions processed by systems operating outside of agreed operational limits may seem harsh, in that some transactions will run successfully. Indeed, this may be the case for as many transactions as were processed before the system reached capacity. There is therefore an argument to say capacity reduction can be ignored. However, its use may encourage more timely capacity management initiatives.

Technology Count

It will not be unusual for the systems you are involved with to comprise a number of technologies or components. A typical server application may well comprise the servers themselves, a content management system and one or more messaging technologies to allow it to communicate to a back-end system. If this is the case, then it seems reasonable to reflect the number of technologies being upgraded in the analysis of the maintenance activity to be undertaken. As you will see later, Green Point Analysis accommodates this by considering the number of technologies maintenance activity impacts.

Perhaps the best way to look at this is by thinking in terms of business and system transactions, or logical and physical transactions. That is to say, a business transaction can be logically viewed as a single event; however when you view this from a physical system perspective, the transaction is a chain of interlinked activities. For example, a user request may be collected on the presentation layer by the content management system, processed by a scripting language on the server and transferred via one or more messaging technologies to a back-end system. This process may involve four or five technologies, all of which could require upgrading.

As mentioned previously with regard to multiple technologies and components, it may well be that the maintenance lives of these technologies are not synchronised. If this is the case, you can take a conservative view and use the maintenance life of the technology that finishes first. Alternatively, you may wish to consider each technology independently.

If the maintenance lives of technologies are not synchronised, and you choose to look at them independently, then your calculations will show a greater number of transactions. Including a higher number of transactions in your Green Point Analysis will result in a greater number of green points being claimed. However, Green Point Analysis is not an exact science and the extra effort and accuracy may not result in significant benefit.

A more valid example for keeping technologies separate would be the case where a maintenance initiative concerns the upgrade of a single technology across a system estate. If only one technology is being maintained, then there is limited value in considering those that are not being touched. In this scenario the whole system may not be brought under support; however maintaining one component will reduce the risk of a failure, if only for one technology in the stack. Considering which of the estate's systems processes the most transactions may therefore be worthwhile.

The concepts discussed in this chapter are illustrated in the diagram below. Many of these were shown in the previous two diagrams. The thing to note here is capacity reduction, which has the effect of shortening the maintenance life. In addition to this, technology count is shown on the z-axis running into the page

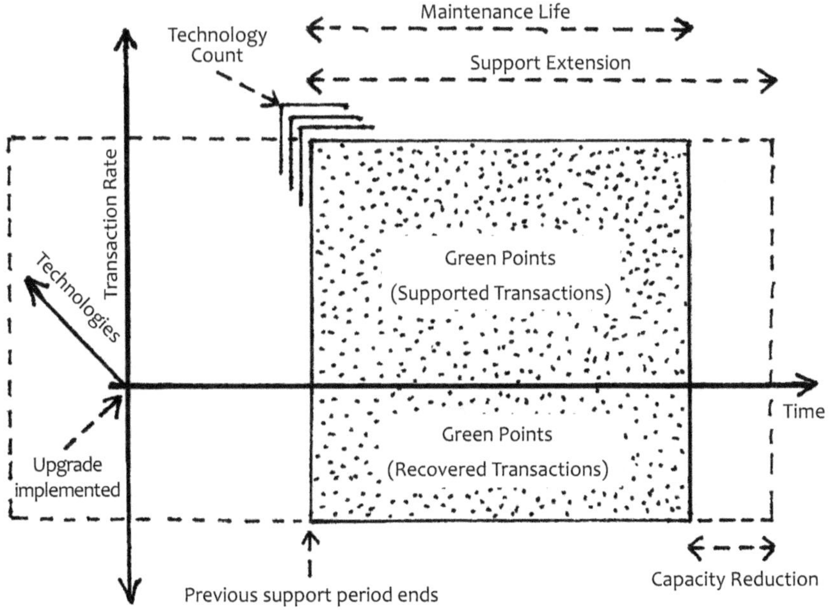

Chapter 8 - Green Point Calculation

Green Point Equations

On first view the equation used to calculate green points looks complex. This is because it contains a lot of arguments (inputs/variables). In essence it's quite simple. We take the maintenance life and multiply this by the transaction rates for both supported and recovered transactions, the transaction ratings having been multiplied by the appropriate weighting coefficients. The only thing to do then is to multiply everything by the technology count.

This chapter details the mathematics used to calculate green points and uses a worked example to demonstrate their application.

Maintenance Life

Before looking at green point calculation, we can work out the maintenance life upfront. This is calculated thus:

Maintenance Life, $t_m = t_s - t_r$
Where:
t_s = Support Extension
t_r = Capacity Reduction

These concepts are described in more detail in Chapter 7.

Green Point Calculation

The equation used to calculate green points follows. Please note this equation will change depending on the weighting coefficients being used.

Green Points, $n_{gp} = n_t \, t_m \, C_T \, C_S \, (r_s \, C_R \, C_A \, C_C + r_r \, C_O)$
Where:
n_t = Number of Technologies
t_m = Maintenance Life
r_s = Supported Transaction Rate
r_r = Recovered Transaction Rate
C_X = Weighting Coefficients

In the above representation of the equation, two of the weighting coefficients have been pulled out of brackets. This is because these coefficients are applied to both recovered and supported transactions. Weighting coefficients can be applied to supported transactions, recovered transactions or both.

If recovered and supported transactions were to be considered separately the equations would look like this:

$$\textbf{Supported Green Points, } n_s = n_t\, t_m\, r_s\, C_T\, C_S\, C_R\, C_A\, C_C$$
$$\textbf{Recovered Green Points, } n_r = n_t\, t_m\, r_r\, C_T\, C_S\, C_O$$

Transaction Rates

The transactions in these equations are expressed as rates. These rates can then be multiplied by the maintenance life to give us the number of transactions at the core of our green point calculation.

The supported transaction rate (r_s) allows us to determine the number of transactions which will be processed during the maintenance life, i.e. the number of transactions processed on a supported system, operating within its design capacity.

The recovered transaction rate (r_r) relates to the number of transactions which are being lost by the system to be maintained. Transactions may not be getting processed for a number of reasons, such as system instability or capacity issues. Recovered transaction rate is derived from an assessment of the existing system and the outages it is experiencing.

Weighting Coefficients

The weighting coefficients used here are as follows:

C_T = Tiering Coefficient [1]
C_R = Refactoring Coefficient [2]
C_A = Architecture Coefficient [2]
C_S = Strategy Coefficient [1]
C_C = Security Coefficient [2]
C_O = Outage Coefficient [3]

Notes:

1. The tiering coefficient (C_T) is applied to both supported and recovered transactions. This is because the tier reflects the importance of the system to the business, therefore whether a transaction is unsupported or being lost it is still important. Similarly, it also makes sense to apply the strategy coefficient, (C_S) to all transactions. If a system supports the business strategy, then the processing of all of its transactions on a supported platform will be desirable.
2. The weighting coefficients of refactoring (C_R), architecture (C_A) and security (C_C) are only applied to supported transactions. If a transaction is lost, it is irrelevant whether or not it would have been processed by a refactored, architecturally strategic and secure platform.
3. The outage coefficient (C_O) is applied to recovered transactions as its purpose is to exaggerate the number of green points claimed by the recovery of lost transactions.

Technology Count

Technology count multiplies the number of green points by the number of technologies or architectural layers you are maintaining. If the maintenance life of technologies is significantly differently, green points can be calculated for each technology as follows:

$$\text{Green Points (Technology 1)} = t_m\, C_T\, C_S\, (r_s\, C_R\, C_A\, C_C + r_r\, C_O)$$
$$\text{Green Points (Technology 2)} = t_m\, C_T\, C_S\, (r_s\, C_R\, C_A\, C_C + r_r\, C_O)$$
$$\text{Green Points} = \text{Green Points (Technology 1)} + \text{Green Points (Technology 2)}$$

Green Points Graphically

By way of a summary, a graphical representation of green point calculation is shown below:

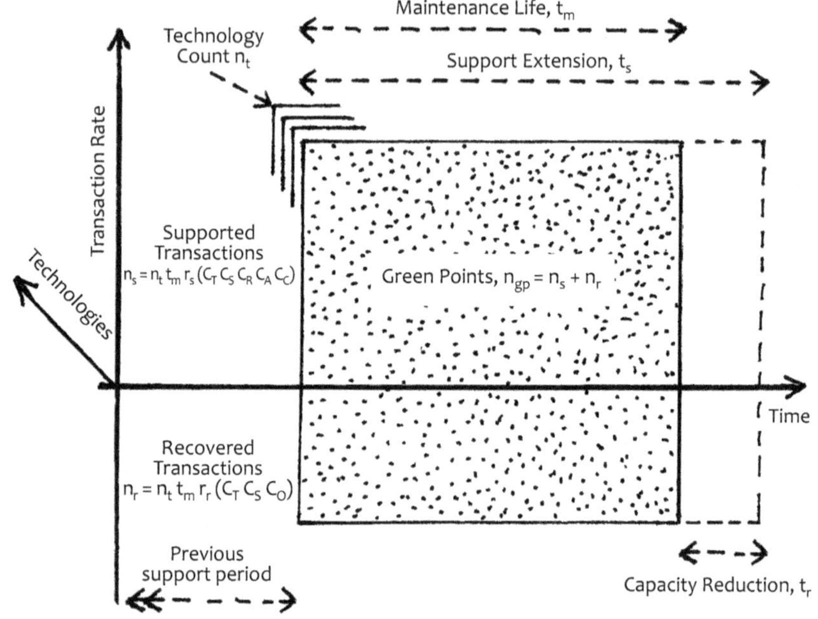

Green Point Calculation

Worked Example

The use of the above equations and coefficients is demonstrated in the following example:

A bank requires an upgrade to its Tier 1 share trading platform. This involves the provision of new physical servers, a refactoring of the application code to remove an obsolete messaging technology and the implementation of new middleware software comprising the web server and two messaging technologies. Please note, the refactoring of the application code is considered minor.

Currently the system is running out of support and the best estimate at this stage of the project is that the upgrade will take six months. The manufacture support for the versions of all the new hardware and middleware will expire three years from the current date. In months where there are no outages, the platform currently processes 40,000 business transactions and no growth is anticipated. Please note, although the system runs well within capacity, it experiences outages averaging three hours a week. This is just outside its service level agreement of 99.99% availability. It is expected that the new technologies will run without outages.

The planned maintenance of the system will not align the application with the bank's strategic architecture; however it will resolve some minor security issues.

First, we calculate the maintenance life. The manufacture support of the new technologies expires in three years' time and the maintenance will take six months to implement. There are no issues with capacity so this will not impact the system's maintenance life. Given the previous support has expired, this is a remediation project and the maintenance life starts on the date the upgrade is implemented.

Maintenance Life, $t_m = t_s - t_r$

Where:

> Support Extension, t_s = 30 months (3 years less 6 months to implement)
> Capacity Reduction, t_r = 0 (No capacity issues expected)
> Maintenance Life, t_m = 30 - 0 = 30 months

Green Points, $n_{gp} = n_t\, t_m\, C_T\, C_S\, (r_s\, C_R\, C_A\, C_C + r_r\, C_O)$

Where:

> Number of Technologies, n_t = 4 (Physical web servers
> & 2 messaging technologies)
> Maintenance Life, t_m = 30 months
> Supported Transaction Rate, r_s = 40,000 transactions per month
> Recovered Transaction Rate, r_r = 40,000 x 3/168 = 714 transactions
> per month
> (NB 168 is the number of hours in a week, 24 hours x 7 days)
> Tiering Coefficient, C_T = 0.8 (Tier 1)
> Refactoring Coefficient, C_R = 1.1 (Minor)
> Architecture Coefficient, C_A = 1.0 (No move to strategic architecture)
> Strategy Coefficient, C_S = 1.0 (Like-for-like migration)
> Security Coefficient, C_C = 1.3 (Minor fixes implemented)
> Outage Coefficient, C_O = 100 (Outside limits)

Green Points, n_{gp}
> = 4 x 30 x 0.8 x 1.0 ((40,000 x 1.1 x 1.0 x 1.3) + (714 x 100))
> = 96 (57,200 + 71,400)
> = 12,345,600 green points

As can be seen from the above the impact of recovered transactions is significant.

Chapter 9 - Applications of Green Point Analysis

Green Point Analysis can be applied in many ways and is useful at project, portfolio and organisation level. A green point is a unit of measurement of the value embedded by the maintenance of information systems. Green points can be used in the comparison of maintenance options, the tracking of the delivery of maintenance initiatives and the monitoring of the ongoing effectiveness of maintenance work. This chapter lists some of the potential applications of Green Point Analysis.

Assessment of Embedded Value

The idea for Green Point Analysis sprang from the thought that there are better ways of expressing the value embedded by the maintenance of information systems than the cost incurred in undertaking it. Earned value management allows us to take the focus away from burn rate and what we have spent and lets us think in terms of what we have delivered. It does not, however, provide a way of assessing the effectiveness of that investment. What we're saying here is you can maintain a system for seventy per cent of the cost of the initial estimate, but if that system does not support a great deal of business activity, has the money been spent wisely?

Green Point Analysis uncouples the maintenance upgrades from a monetary measure and instead provides a currency for the value embedded by maintenance and remediation activity called a green point. In doing so it provides a method for tracking the amount of value being delivered by the effort and investment you are making.

Let's elaborate on this by way of an example and consider a scenario in which you have been allocated an annual budget to maintain an information system estate. The first thing you and your team do is perform some initial analysis to determine which systems require maintenance in the coming year and formulate this into a programme of projects to be delivered throughout the course of the period.

What would be useful here is a way of tracking and reporting progress as you work through the year. If you use Green Point Analysis to determine how many green points each project delivery claims, you have a metric to track your progress against plan, i.e. if at the beginning of the year you commit to delivering a particular number of green points and by half year you are fifty per cent of the way there, then you would appear to be on track. If you have achieved this having only spent a third of your budget, even better; you may even be able to release some of your budget for use elsewhere.

It's worth noting that as you work your way through the year and your knowledge of both your project portfolio and implementation of Green Point Analysis evolves, you may decide to make some adjustments in the way you are calculating your green points. For example, there may be a particular weighting coefficient that is exaggerating the number of green points claimed by some projects a little more than you feel appropriate. If this is the case, it is perfectly acceptable to make a tweak to your Green Point Analysis approach, as long as this tweak is applied across the whole portfolio.

If you do decide to adjust your green point calculation, you need to be aware of how this is communicated to stakeholders outside the programme team. Should you state at the beginning of the year that you will be delivering 900,000 green points and this drops to 800,000 then the perception will be that you are delivering less than you set out to. Perhaps the best way to remove this potential confusion is to express your green point delivery as a percentage in communications external to the programme.

The following graph provides a simple representation of how a programme of work may claim green points throughout its duration:

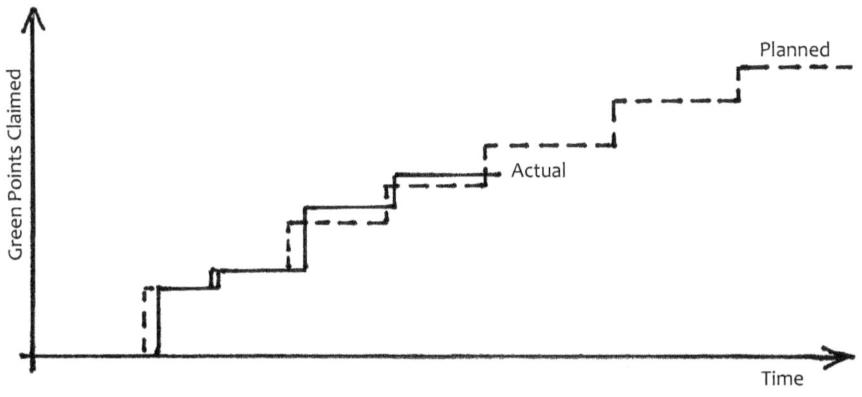

Green Points Claimed (Planned Versus Actual)

Relative Scoring for Prioritisation

Seasoned portfolio, programme and project managers will be aware that initiatives are often constrained by time, people and budgets; consequently senior stakeholders are often called upon to make prioritisation calls. When it comes to deciding where to allocate your resources, Green Point Analysis provides a useful metric.

By way of an example let's take a simple scenario where you are considering which one of two projects to progress, each estimated at around £500,000. If Green Point Analysis shows one project claiming 200,000 more green points than the other, then you may well decide to tackle this one first.

Alternatively, you may have two projects of unequal values. If so, you could calculate the monetary cost of claiming the green points on the respective projects as follows:

$$\textbf{Green Point Cost = Estimated Cost / Green Points}$$

Project	Estimated Cost	Green Points	Green Point Cost
A	£500,000	1,600,000	£0.32
B	£750,000	2,000,000	£0.38

In this example, Project A will embed less value, in that it will allow you to claim less green points; however the number of green points that can be claimed will be cheaper. Please note, the estimated cost should be the whole life cost including the cost of both the maintenance and the system's subsequent operation until the end of the maintenance life of the upgrade.

When it comes to prioritisation, the use of Green Point Analysis should serve to take out some of the emotion regarding what takes precedence. It could be that the projects under consideration serve different stakeholders, with each thinking the maintenance of their systems should take priority. The mathematics involved in Green Point Analysis will probably not totally convince everyone, however it will give a quantitative assessment to feed into discussions.

Finally, you may be asked to consider the inclusion of new work in the scope of the programme. If so, Green Point Analysis will provide a quick way to determine how a new piece of work slots into your existing list of priorities. If the new piece of work claims a sizable amount of green points, it may well be prudent to prioritise the new piece of work over that which is in progress. In this scenario the investment in the ongoing project would be taken as the estimate of the whole life cost from that point, i.e. the estimate to complete the maintenance plus the operation costs.

Renew Or Refurbish Assessments

There comes a point in the life of most things when the cost of maintenance becomes uneconomical. It is not always easy to understand when this point has been reached.

If we assume that the maintenance life of a refurbished system is less than building a new one, then it makes sense to try to understand the value embedded by each approach. A simplistic approach would be to divide the whole life cost of each option by its respective maintenance life to determine the cost per year. This approach will not, however, reflect any nuances in the quality of service delivered by a new as opposed to a refurbished system. If we consider some of the weighting coefficients used in Green Point Analysis, it may be that these take different values depending on the options you are considering. The new-build option could align better with the organisation's strategic architecture and better support the business strategy. Alternatively, a new system might perform better in respect of security and outages.

If there are significant differences in the available options, then Green Point Analysis will provide a quantitative analysis. If the maintenance lives of the options are different, then comparison of green point cost should be made, i.e. the estimate of whole life cost divided by number of green points claimed.

Build, Buy Or Lease Assessments

Green Point Analysis is also useful when considering the approach to extending the life of a service delivered by a system. Consider a scenario where there are three solutions for the replacement of an aging system: a bespoke system could be built from scratch, a proprietary system could be purchased or a system could be leased, such as in the example of a cloud solution. Each of these options will have different costs and probably different maintenance life lengths. More relevantly, each solution is likely to differ with respect to how closely it meets your requirements and specification. You would hope a system built from scratch would be a good match to the requirements and specification. If so, it should perform well against the criteria rated by weighting coefficients and consequently do well when it comes to claiming green points. It is likely, however, that building a system will also be the most expensive option.

As we have discussed previously, green point cost can be used to assess whether there is value in making this additional investment over choosing one of the off-the-shelf options, green point cost being the estimated whole life cost of an option divided by the number of green points it can claim.

Budget Reductions

From time to time one will be asked to cut one's coat according to one's cloth, i.e. you will be asked to cancel some projects to meet the challenge of reductions in budget. Ideally, you would be able to achieve the target budget reduction by not starting planned work; however if this is not enough, you will then need to turn your gaze to in-flight projects. If this is the case, then green point cost will be useful in deciding what does and does not get the chop.

When using green point cost to analyse the benefit of completing works in progress, the cost of green points is calculated using estimate to complete. In doing so projects nearing completion, with less budget yet to spend, will tend to demonstrate good value from a green point cost perspective.

High-level Estimating

As your usage of Green Point Analysis becomes more mature and you build up an archive of completed projects, you will have a record of how much it is costing you to claim each green point, i.e. the green point cost mentioned earlier. If you are managing to achieve some consistency in green point cost, then you have a useful metric for use in high-level estimating that is both quick and simple to apply. The project cost is estimated thus:

High-level Estimate = Green Points x Green Point Cost

The thing to note here is that this is an analogous estimating technique, and consequently its accuracy is dependent on how alike the work you are planning is to the examples from which you are taking your green point cost metric. The closer the initiatives are with respect to overall size and blend of technologies, the more accurate this type of estimating should be. When it comes to estimating, it is therefore beneficial to treat technologies separately for both the collection of green point cost metrics and the estimating itself. By doing so, the data you collect will be more useful when used to estimate different software stacks.

If you did keep an archive of historical projects and recorded the time it took to deliver this work, then you would also have a metric useful in the analogous estimating of project timelines and cost. The calculation would be thus:

High-level Timeline = Green Points x Green Point Rate

It should be noted that analogous estimating techniques, such as the one described here, are only appropriate for high-level estimates used in the early stages of project planning. It is therefore recommended that estimates are subsequently refined using techniques that consider the work involved, rather than the general nature of the system you are maintaining.

Quantification Of Incremental Improvement

Pick up any book on either business or project management and there will likely be a mention of incremental improvement. As with most things, there will be opportunities to refine the way you maintain your systems. If this is the case then Green Point Analysis provides a tool to help you track any improvement you make. Again, the metric we use is that of green point cost. If this is tracked from project to project and the trend is for it to reduce then it is reasonable to assume that there is a correlation between this and your organisation getting better at maintaining its systems.

Tracking green point cost may also serve to highlight when the investment in maintaining your systems is not achieving the benefits it once did and you have reached a point of diminishing returns, where your maintenance activity tends to involve more work than makes economic and practical sense. It should be noted that a rise in green point cost may also indicate that a system has reached the end of its working life and is ready for decommissioning. Green point cost will rise both when a system is processing fewer and fewer transactions, and when it becomes more expensive to maintain the antiquated technology it comprises.

Audit/Investment Tracking

The nature of maintenance work is such that there is likely to be competition for budget challenges with projects initiated to increase revenue. If it is that the balance between change and maintenance is adjusted in either direction then it should be useful to understand the impact of this in terms of system health, number/length of outages. If you know how many green points are being delivered along with the number and length of outages you are experiencing, then you may be able to see a correlation.

Note the terminology here. We are talking about green points 'delivered' and not 'claimed'. Green points are claimed at the point a maintenance project is implemented; however the benefit of a supported transaction, the event at the core of a green point, is not seen until that transaction is processed at some point during the course of the maintenance life of the system.

A project might claim three million green points, but with respect to audit and tracking you need to consider when these are actually delivered, i.e. if the maintenance life of the project is three years, it will deliver a million green points a year towards your annual total.

The graph below illustrates a scenario where the effort expended on maintenance is reducing. Consequently, some of the systems of the system estate are now out of support and the delivery of green points is declining. Although there is no real correlation between green points delivered and the number of outages, the reduced support level is causing an increase in the typical length of the outages and lost service time.

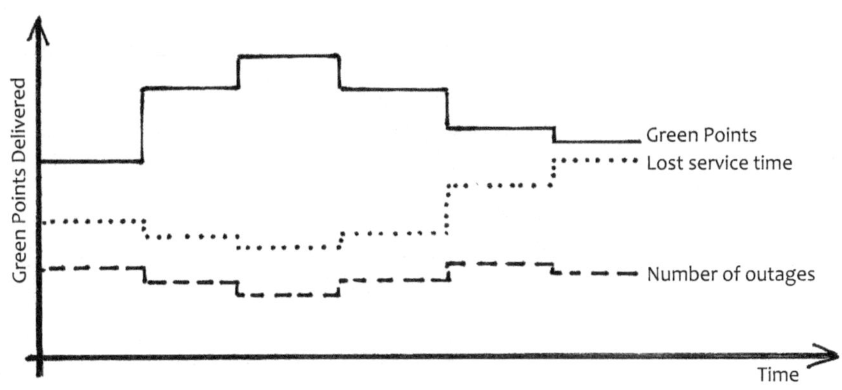

Maintenance Tracking Using Green Point Delivery

Chapter 10 - System Health

The following chapter is perhaps somewhat of an aside, in that it is not directly related to Green Point Analysis. It presents an idea on how you might analyse and communicate the health of your system estate by focusing on some of the same system characteristics you consider when selecting the weighting coefficients used in Green Point Analysis. It should, however, be noted that not all of these characteristics referenced by weighting coefficients are applicable to the assessment of system health. For example, if we look at weighting coefficients used in the examples in this book, then a system's tier is not a characteristic that concerns its health. It may well be that tier is an important consideration for those systems in poor health; however it is not a measure of system health in itself. Note, there is no real need to aim for consistency between the system characteristics focused on by weighting coefficients and those used to assess system health.

At this point let's introduce a new concept, that of a 'health lens'. A health lens is a characteristic of a system, the evaluation of which examines an aspect of system health and ultimately contributes to the overall assessment of a system's health.

Example Health Lenses

Some example health lenses are described below. A test is shown against each lens to show how it may be evaluated:

Health Lenses	Test
Support Lens * (H_U)	Does the system have sufficient vendor support and licensing arrangements in place? Note that with regards to remaining support life it may be useful to define a minimum period against which to assess this lens.
Outage Lens (H_O)	Does the level of resilience and disaster recovery reduce outages below agreed levels of service?
Security Lens (H_C)	Are there any known security vulnerabilities or outstanding services packs/patches requiring implementation?
Architecture Lens (H_A)	Is the system running on strategic technology platforms and thus realising the sustainable cost savings achieved through rationalisation?
Growth Lens * (H_G)	Does the system have sufficient capacity to accommodate the anticipated future growth?
Strategy Lens (H_S)	Does the system support the current business strategy?

Health Lenses	Test
Refactoring Lens (H_R)	Would the system benefit from the refactoring of application code to improve maintainability with respect to both troubleshooting and functional improvements?

* Note, the lenses/characteristics do not map to weighting coefficients as such, however they are embedded in other aspects of Green Point Analysis.

Health Lens Aggregation

Once you have decided on your health lenses you will need a way of aggregating the related analysis in order to produce an overall picture of system health. There are at least two ways of doing this; you could view each health lens test as a pass or fail, or you could implement a scoring system that gauges the degree of a system's compliance to each test. If you do go down the scoring route you might wish to weight the scoring you give to the lenses that are of the most concern.

System Health Classification

Finally let's have a non-numeric way of classifying the system. We could go down the route of RAG (red/amber/green) status and classify systems in good health green and those in poor health red, i.e. those performing well against the health lenses would gain a green classification.

Given that RAG status is generally used to communicate programme and project status, let's not use it. Instead, let's classify our systems as gold, silver or bronze, with systems not meeting the bronze standard categorised as unclassified.

Sticking with a pass/fail assessment you then need to decide how the passing of a lens test maps to achieving a particular classification. An example of how this might be done is shown below. This might seem peculiar at first, in that passing the tests relating to what may be considered the more important system characteristics will result in only a bronze classification.

	Classification		
Health Lens/Test	**Bronze**	**Silver**	**Gold**
Support Lens (H_u)	✓	✓	✓
Outage Lens (H_O)	✓	✓	✓
Security Lens (H_c)	✓	✓	✓
Architecture Lens (H_A)		✓	✓
Growth Lens (H_G)		✓	✓
Strategy Lens (H_S)			✓
Refactoring Lens (H_R)			✓

What the previous table is telling you is that to achieve a bronze classification the system needs to pass the top three tests, for silver the top five and for gold all seven assessments.

If you choose a scoring approach you will need to decide the score required to achieve each classification. The problem with this is that you may have an issue with an important lens, but still score well enough on the others to give what looks to be a good rating. For example, a system with a security vulnerability may still score well enough on the other health lens tests to give it a silver or perhaps even a gold classification.

Chapter 11 - Conclusion

Green points and Green Point Analysis equip those who understand the importance of information system maintenance with a technique to ensure investment in system maintenance is directed efficiently. This technique provides a metric for the value added by maintenance activities, which recognises that the work done by some systems is of greater business benefit than that done by others. In addition to this, the weighting coefficients used by Green Point Analysis accommodate the competing priorities of people employed in different roles across an organisation.

The green point metric is useful at both project and enterprise-level. It provides a quantitative method for assessing maintenance and remediation options and a way to monitor and track project performance and progress using a metric in addition to the cost involved in undertaking this work. At an organisation level, Green Point Analysis allows managers to monitor the ongoing effectiveness of the maintenance work performed across a portfolio of projects.

The insight provided by green points is of interest to stakeholders working in different roles across an organisation. These include systems analysts, portfolio, programme and project managers, development managers, product owners, service owners and business sponsors. Collectively, these people have an interest in the stable operation of the technology that supports the products and services delivered by their company.

Given the large sums invested on information systems, it is important to ensure the maximum benefit is gained from this outlay. Effective system maintenance serves to insure this investment by ensuring an organisation's systems are robust and highly-available. In the digital age, information systems are integral to a customer's experience of an organisation. Poorly-maintained, under-performing systems will have a detrimental effect on your organisation's reputation and the company's brand. Establishing a valued brand requires a lot of effort and expense. It is important to protect this investment.

If you would like help in using green points to improve the effectiveness of your system maintenance initiatives, get in touch now via the Green Points™ website, GreenPts.org

If you've found this book useful, please consider leaving a short review on Amazon.

Appendices

Appendix A: Data Sheets

Equations

Maintenance Life	Maintenance Life, $t_m = t_s - t_r$ Where: $\quad t_s$ = Support Extension $\quad t_r$ = Capacity Reduction
Supported Transactions	Supported Transactions, $n_s = n_t\, t_m\, r_s$ Where: $\quad n_t$ = Number of Technologies $\quad t_m$ = Maintenance Life $\quad r_s$ = Supported Transaction Rate
Recovered Transactions	Recovered Transactions, $n_r = n_t\, t_m\, r_r$ Where: $\quad n_t$ = Number of Technologies $\quad t_m$ = Maintenance Life $\quad r_r$ = Recovered Transaction Rate
Total Transactions	Total Transactions, $n_t = n_s + n_r$ Where: $\quad n_s$ = Supported Transactions $\quad n_r$ = Recovered Transactions
T-shirt Sizing	Supported Transactions = Number of Users x Typical Usage Factor x Transactions per Session
Green Point Calculation	Green Points, $n_{gp} = n_t\, t_m\, C_T\, C_S\, (r_s\, C_R\, C_A\, C_C + r_r\, C_O)$ Where: $\quad n_t$ = Number of Technologies $\quad t_m$ = Maintenance Life $\quad r_s$ = Supported Transaction Rate $\quad r_r$ = Recovered Transaction Rate $\quad C_T$ = Tiering Coefficient $\quad C_R$ = Refactoring Coefficient $\quad C_A$ = Architecture Coefficient $\quad C_S$ = Strategy Coefficient $\quad C_C$ = Security Coefficient $\quad C_O$ = Outage Coefficient
Green Point Cost	Green Point Cost = Estimated Cost / Green Points
High-level Estimating	High-level Estimate = Green Points x Green Point Cost
High-level Planning	High-level Time Span = Green Points x Green Point Rate

Example Weighting Coefficients

Coefficient	Suggested Values
Tiering Coefficient (C_T)	Tier 0 = 1.0 Tier 1 = 0.8 Tier 2 = 0.5 Tier 3 = 0.2
Refactoring Coefficient (C_R)	None = 1.0 Very minor = 1.05 Minor = 1.1 Major = 1.2 Very major = 1.4
Architecture Coefficient (C_A)	System will move away from strategic architecture = 0.5 System stays on non-strategic architecture = 0.9 System uses strategic architecture = 1.0 System will move to strategic architecture = 1.2
Strategy Coefficient (C_S)	No alignment with business strategy = 1.0 Weak alignment with business strategy = 1.05 Reasonable alignment with business strategy = 1.1 Strong alignment with business strategy = 1.25 Very strong alignment with business strategy = 1.5
Security Coefficient (C_C)	No fixes implemented = 1.0 Very minor fixes implemented = 1.1 Minor fixes implemented = 1.3 Major fixes implemented = 1.6 Very major fixes implemented = 2.0
Outage Coefficient (C_O)	Resilience/disaster recovery within agreed limits = 1 Resilience/disaster recovery outside agreed limits = 100

Green Points Graphically

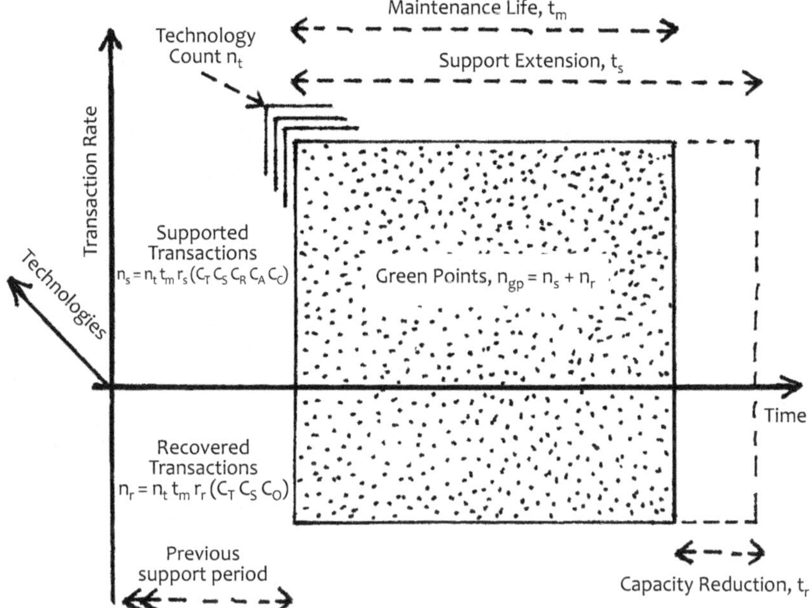

Green Point Calculation

Appendix B: The Coffee Shop Example

The following example describes the application of Green Point Analysis to a non-information system scenario. Green point calculation is presented in this manner in order to avoid distractions where the example given differs from a similar scenario that might be found in your organisation.

The Coffee Shop Story

In order to decouple Green Point Analysis from any pre-existing views of what information systems are, let's consider a scenario that definitely isn't directly related to information systems. Let's imagine you own three coffee shops and have decided to update the coffee-making equipment in order that you can maintain the high quality of the tasty beverage you serve your customers.

The number of cups of coffee typically served in each of your outlets is shown below:

Coffee Shop Square = 500 cups per day
Coffee Shop Circle = 400 cups per day
Coffee Shop Triangle = 250 cups per day

Now let's put some reality around this completely made-up example. You may wish to update all the equipment immediately; however from the perspective of cash flowing through your organisation it could make better sense to upgrade one outlet every six months. Consequently, you need to prioritise. Given the information you have at present, this looks quite straightforward. We can give priority to the outlet serving the most cups of coffee. If we do this we would look to upgrade Coffee Shop Square, followed by Circle and finally Triangle.

The problem with this approach is that we haven't considered the age of the equipment. It may be that the equipment in Coffee Shop Square is newer than the kit in the other stores and therefore in less need of an upgrade. In order that we may better understand the relevance of the equipment's age, let us give it a design life, a period in which the equipment is under warranty and therefore supported by the manufacturer. For the sake of argument, we will take this as five years. At this point we will also define a term for a cup of coffee served within the warranty period, namely a 'supported transaction'.

To extend our example, the ages of the equipment in the respective coffee shops are as follows:

Coffee Shop Square = 3 years old
Coffee Shop Circle = 4 years old
Coffee Shop Triangle = 5 years old

In the case of Coffee Shop Square, the warranty still has two years to run (the five-year period of the warranty less the age of the equipment). Consequently, if we were to upgrade this kit now, we would only be benefiting to the tune of three additional years of manufacture support. If we consider this along with the number of cups of coffee served in this period we can determine the benefit of making this investment, i.e. the number of additional supported transactions.

The calculation of supported transactions is a simple one:

Supported Transactions = (Warranty Period - Remaining Warranty Period) x Transaction Rate
Coffee Shop Square = (5 years - (5 - 3) years) x 365 days x 500 transactions per day
= 547,500 supported transactions
Coffee Shop Circle = (5 years - (5 - 4) years) x 365 days x 400 transactions per day
= 584,000 supported transactions
Coffee Shop Triangle = (5 years - (5 - 5) years) x 365 days x 250 transactions per day
= 456,250 supported transactions
Total (if upgrades performed concurrently) = 1,587,750 supported transactions

Given the above, we have a different picture. It may be marginal; however, it appears that the Coffee Shop Circle should take priority. If we now revise the priority to Circle, Square then Triangle, and persist with the assumption that upgrades will be performed at six-monthly intervals, we have the below.

Note, the age of Square has been increased by 0.5 years to reflect its age at the time of the upgrade six months in the future. The age of Triangle is actually irrelevant, in that any delay will put it out of support and therefore the whole period of the warranty is considered. More of this later.

Coffee Shop Square
    = (5 years - (5 - 3.5) years) x 365 days x 500 transactions per day
    = 638,750 supported transactions
Coffee Shop Circle
    = (5 years - (5 - 4) years) x 365 days x 400 transactions per day
    = 584,000 supported transactions
Coffee Shop Triangle
    = 5 years x 365 days x 250 transactions per day
    = 456,250 supported transactions
Total = 1,679,000 supported transactions

As you can see, with respect to supported transactions, it appears to be beneficial to prioritise the upgrades in this manner. Clearly this is a result of delaying the upgrade to Coffee Shop Square in order to extend the effect of the cover provided by the existing warranty period. The other thing worthy of note in this scenario is that as Coffee Shop Triangle is at the end of its warranty and is planned to be upgraded last, there is a period of a year where it will be running with no manufacturer support. The consequences of this may not seem great, but it does seem advisable not to have equipment running out of support and there is therefore a case to put Coffee Shop Triangle to the front of the queue. This leaves us with Triangle, Circle, Square, and revises the calculation thus:

Coffee Shop Square
    = (5 years - (5 - 4) years) x 365 days x 500 transactions per day
    = 730,000 supported transactions
Coffee Shop Circle
    = (5 years - (5 - 4.5) years) x 365 days x 400 transactions per day
    = 657,000 supported transactions
Coffee Shop Triangle
    = (5 years - (5 - 5) years) x 365 days x 250 transactions per day
    = 456,250 supported transactions
Total = 1,843,250 supported transactions

As with the previous example, the delay in the number of supported transactions has increased. Again, this is due to the delaying of the upgrades and the extension of the benefit gained from the existing warranties. Clearly the scenario that would result in the most supported transactions is one in which the upgrades are left until just before the warranty expires. To maintain the validity of the example we can assume there is a constraint preventing this, such as financial benefits in taking delivery of the new kit within a particular time period.

This example can be extended further if we consider variations in the transactions themselves, i.e. the types of coffee being sold. If, by some bizarre quirk of geography, the types of coffee sold in each location vary significantly, you may wish to factor this in. The obvious way to do this is to use a monetary value, specifically the profit generated by the sale of each type of coffee; however, for reasons that should become apparent later, let's not do this. Instead, let's reflect this by applying a factor that increases or lessens the relevance of a supported transaction. Effectively we are overstating or understating the effect of a supported transaction in order to reflect its value to the business. In the context of this example we will call this the Profit Coefficient (C_p). The use of words such as 'coefficient' may lead you to think this is starting to get complicated, but it really isn't. The maths is very simple.

For the sake of this example, the Profit Coefficient can take one of three values as follows:

Regular, C_p = 1.0
Premium, C_p = 1.25
Super Premium, C_p = 1.5

Building on the previous calculation we will define our coffee shops of Square, Circle and Triangle as Regular, Premium and Super Premium respectively to give us the following:

Coffee Shop Square
    = 730,000 supported transactions x 1.0 = 730,000 green points
Coffee Shop Circle
    = 657,000 supported transactions x 1.25 = 821,250 green points
Coffee Shop Triangle
    = 456,250 supported transactions x 1.5 = 684,375 green points

The thing to note here is that we are no longer talking in terms of calculating 'supported transactions' but rather 'green points'. Once we have applied a multiplying factor, or coefficient, to a supported transaction it becomes something else. The name given to this something else is a green point, as defined in this guide:

A transaction to which a weighting factor or coefficient has been applied to reflect its business value.

Previously we steered away from talking in terms of monetary values, such as the profit generated by the sale of a cup of coffee. The reason for this is there may be less tangible factors to consider. For example, there could be a variation in the number of customer complaints across your portfolio of coffee shops. 'Complaint' is a very negative word so to reflect this let's introduce a Customer Service Coefficient (C_S). What we are suggesting here is the support of a transaction is critical to providing good customer service. This seems reasonable in that it's hard to argue you are providing a good level of service if you are using dilapidated, poorly maintained equipment. We are also making the perhaps more tenuous suggestion that level of customer service becomes more relevant when customer complaints are more numerous, i.e. that improved customer service correlates to a reduction in customer complaints. This would probably be true in the event that poorly maintained equipment was more likely to break down.

Customer Service Coefficient can take one of three values as follows:

Standard, $C_S = 1.0$
Enhanced, $C_S = 1.1$
Exceptional, $C_S = 1.2$

Green points are now calculated as follows:

Green Points = Supported Transactions x C_P x C_S
Where:
C_P = Profit Coefficient
C_S = Customer Service Coefficient

In the case of our example we will define the level of service appropriate to our coffee shops of Square, Circle and Triangle as Standard, Enhanced and Exceptional respectively. The revised green point calculation is shown below:

Coffee Shop Square = 730,000 x 1.0 x 1.0 = 730,000 green points
Coffee Shop Circle = 657,000 x 1.25 x 1.1 = 903,375 green points
Coffee Shop Triangle = 456,250 x 1.5 x 1.2 = 821,250 green points

… and there we have the essence of green points. They provide a quantifiable metric for use in the decision-making involved in directing investment in maintenance activities. As can be seen from the coffee shop example, where operating outside warranty was considered undesirable, there are other inputs to this decision-making. Green points are also conceptual. The green points used in the analysis of your coffee shop empire are a different currency to those used by your friend when planning the upgrade of his gym equipment. They are designed for use within an organisation and to be useful both in the consideration of options across a project, programme or portfolio, and, if applied consistently, to provide additional insight with respect to both the level of investment in maintenance and the ongoing effectiveness of maintenance activities. As we will see later, if the cost of achieving a green point is calculated and tracked over time, then the effectiveness of maintenance activities within an organisation can be monitored. Conversely, green points are also useful in identifying when the benefit realised from investing in maintenance begins to diminish.

Appendix C: Case Studies

The following case studies are presented to provide examples demonstrating the use of Green Point Analysis. They do not represent cases taken from actual projects or organisations.

1. Embedded Value Assessment

A multimedia company wishes to upgrade the middleware of components of the websites it operates and maintains. This work involves the upgrade of ten server clusters and it is estimated this programme of upgrades will take three years. Given the duration of this initiative, the programme manager wants a way of demonstrating the benefit the maintenance work is delivering throughout the course of the programme. In doing so they believe they will be better equipped to negotiate the department's budget in subsequent years of the programme.

Given that the service clusters were introduced at different times the three middleware components involved in the upgrades vary with respect to the versions they are running on across the system estate. Some initial analysis has been undertaken, the results of which are shown below. The upgrades have been prioritised so that the clusters running the older technology are upgraded first. Note that all the clusters run well within capacity and no appreciable growth is anticipated, therefore Capacity Reduction (t_r) is taken as zero.

	Current Support Expiry Month	Planned Upgrade Month	New Support Expiry Month	Supported Transaction Rate, r_s (per month)	Recovered Transaction Rate, r_r (per month)	Support Extension, t_s (months)
Cluster 1	12	5	60	90,000	0	48
Cluster 2	12	8	60	75,000	100	48
Cluster 3	12	11	60	110,000	0	48
Cluster 4	18	14	60	130,000	0	42
Cluster 5	18	17	60	95,000	200	42
Cluster 6	18	20	60	100,000	0	40
Cluster 7	33	23	60	125,000	0	27
Cluster 8	33	26	60	110,000	0	27
Cluster 9	33	29	60	85,000	500	27
Cluster 10	33	32	60	135,000	0	27

To calculate Support Extension (r_s) we need to consider the date at which this period starts. If the upgrade occurs before the current support arrangement expires, then this will be the end date of the current support. If not, the start date is the date at which the upgrade is implemented. Obviously, the end date of the Support Extension is the date of the new support's expiry.

Note that with respect to Cluster 6 the current support expires before the upgrade is implemented. There is therefore a period when this cluster is running out of support. We therefore have an exposure to the business that should be logged as an issue and communicated to the appropriate stakeholders.

After further analysis and discussion, the following weighting coefficients were agreed. Note, the range of weighting coefficient values used here is that quoted in Chapter 5.

	Tiering Coefficient C_T	Refactoring Coefficient C_R	Architecture Coefficient C_A	Strategy Coefficient C_S	Security Coefficient C_C	Outage Coefficient C_O
Cluster 1	Tier 0 1.0	None 1.0	Move To 1.2	Reasonable 1.1	Minor Fix 1.3	Within Limits 1
Cluster 2	Tier 1 0.8	None 1.0	Move To 1.2	Reasonable 1.1	Minor Fix 1.3	Within Limits 1
Cluster 3	Tier 2 0.5	None 1.0	Move To 1.2	Reasonable 1.1	Minor Fix 1.3	Within Limits 1
Cluster 4	Tier 1 0.8	None 1.0	On 1.0	Strong 1.25	V Minor Fix 1.1	Within Limits 1
Cluster 5	Tier 1 0.8	None 1.0	On 1.0	Strong 1.25	V Minor Fix 1.1	Within Limits 1
Cluster 6	Tier 1 0.8	None 1.0	On 1.0	Strong 1.25	V Minor Fix 1.1	Within Limits 1
Cluster 7	Tier 1 0.8	None 1.0	On 1.0	Strong 1.25	No Fixes 1.0	Within Limits 1

	Tiering Coefficient C_T	Refactoring Coefficient C_R	Architecture Coefficient C_A	Strategy Coefficient C_S	Security Coefficient C_C	Outage Coefficient C_O
Cluster 8	Tier 0	None	On	Strong	No Fixes	Within Limits
	1.0	1.0	1.0	1.25	1.0	1
Cluster 9	Tier 1	None	On	Strong	No Fixes	Outside Limits
	0.8	1.0	1.0	1.25	1.0	100
Cluster 10	Tier 1	None	On	Strong	No Fixes	Within Limits
	0.8	1.0	1.0	1.25	1.0	1

The following points are worth noting:

- Systems of equivalent tiers are hosted on the same cluster. This simplifies things as we don't need to perform our Green Point Analysis on each system.

- There are no changes to the application therefore the refactoring coefficient is 1.0 in all cases.

- The older technologies used by Clusters 1 to 3 do not align with the strategic architecture. This will be addressed by the upgrade and is therefore reflected in the values taken by the architecture coefficient. It may be that there has been a change in the preferred operating system and/or web server since these clusters were last upgraded.

- There are some security issues with the older implementations that will be rectified by this programme. This can be seen from the values taken by the security coefficient. These issues have been rated as requiring minor and very minor fixes for Clusters 1 to 3 and 4 to 6 respectively.

- Although Clusters 2, 5 and 9 are experiencing outages, it is only Cluster 9 that is breaching its service level agreement. The failure to operate within agreed limits is reflected in the outage coefficient.

The number of green points claimed by the maintenance of each cluster is determined as follows:

i)   Calculate Maintenance Life

Maintenance Life, $t_m = t_s - t_r$

Note, given that no capacity issues are expected within the period of the Support Extension then the Capacity Reduction factor t_r is 0 and $t_m = t_s$.

ii) Calculate Green Points

Green Points, $n_{gp} = n_t \, t_m \, C_T \, C_S \, (r_s \, C_R \, C_A \, C_C + r_r \, C_O)$

All the figures required by this formula are included in the tables above, except for Number of Technologies, $n_t = 3$

	Maintenance Life $t_m = t_s - t_r$	Green Points $n_{gp} = n_t \, t_m \, C_T \, C_S \, (r_s \, C_R \, C_A \, C_C + r_r \, C_O)$
Cluster 1	48	22,239,360
Cluster 2	48	14,838,912
Cluster 3	48	13,590,720
Cluster 4	42	18,018,000
Cluster 5	42	13,192,200
Cluster 6	40	13,200,000
Cluster 7	27	10,125,000
Cluster 8	27	11,137,500
Cluster 9	27	10,935,000
Cluster 10	27	10,530,000

The graph below shows the status of the programme after one year:

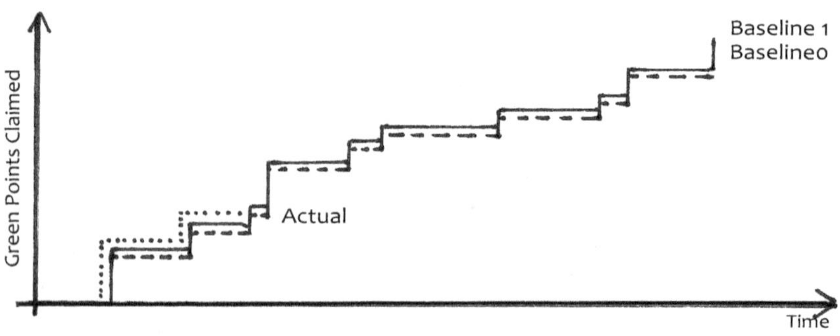

Green Point Delivery Tracker

Note the difference between the two baseline plans is due to the release of a new version of middleware occurring around the time Cluster 3 was implemented, which extended the maintenance life by a further 12 months.

2. Prioritisation Assessment

A hosting services provider hosts a suite of client sites across six server farms located in each of its two data centres. The data centres operate hot-cold with all the services it hosts running out of a primary site and the secondary site providing contingency in the event of a serious issue in the primary location.

The middleware the server farms run on is in need of a technology refresh. It comprises four components and maintenance was last performed two years ago with the server farms being upgraded at monthly intervals. The current support will expire in 12 months. The proposed upgrade will extend support by 12 months; however it is expected that the system estate will start experiencing capacity issues six months before the end of this period. The number of transactions processed by each farm is available from system logs.

In order that each client is treated fairly, the data centre manager would like the order in which the upgrades are performed to be prioritised using a mathematical assessment. Green Point Analysis has been chosen to perform this assessment.

Given that each server farm is an instance of the same proposition there is little variance across the farms. The elements that do vary are listed below; of these the most notable is the tiering coefficient, which reflects the differing levels of service offered by the hosting provider.

	Supported Transaction Rate r_s (per month)	Recovered Transaction Rate r_r (per month)	Tiering Coefficient C_T	Outage Coefficient C_O
Farm Blue Bell	100,000	100	Tier 0 1.0	Outside Limits 100
Farm Carrsides	90,000	150	Tier 0 1.0	Outside Limits 100
Farm Dovecote	95,000	50	Tier 1 0.8	Within Limits 1
Farm Leechmire	95,000	100	Tier 1 0.8	Within Limits 1
Farm Owington	105,000	75	Tier 2 0.5	Within Limits 1
Farm Sheraton	85,000	0	Tier 2 0.5	Within Limits 1

The other parameters used in the Green Point Analysis are defined below:

Support Extension, t_s = 36 months (48 months new - 12 months current)
Capacity Reduction, t_r = 6 months

Number of Technologies, n_t = 4
Maintenance Life, $t_m = t_s - t_r$ = 36 - 6 = 30 months

Supported Transaction Rate, r_s (See table)
Recovered Transaction Rate, r_r (See table)

Tiering Coefficient, C_T (See table)
Refactoring Coefficient, C_R = 1.0 (None)
Architecture Coefficient, C_A = 1.0 (Systems use strategic architecture)
Strategy Coefficient, C_S = 1.25 (Strong alignment)
Security Coefficient, C_C = 1.0 (No fixes implemented)
Outage Coefficient, C_O (See table)

The number of green points claimed by each farm is shown below:

	Green Points $n_{gp} = n_t\, t_m\, C_T\, C_S\, (r_s\, C_R\, C_A\, C_C + r_r\, C_O)$
Farm Blue Bell	16,500,000
Farm Carrsides	15,750,000
Farm Dovecote	11,406,000
Farm Leechmire	11,412,000
Farm Owington	7,880,625
Farm Sheraton	6,375,000

As can be seen from the green points claimed by the maintenance, the suggested prioritisation should remain as listed with the exception of Leechmire, which should take precedence over Dovecote. Note that as the start of the support extension period is taken as the end date of the current support, reprioritisation of the upgrades will not affect the green point weighting.

3. Build, Buy Or Lease Assessment

A start-up company is considering the options for its accounting systems. An internal discussion with the team has produced three potential options: a bespoke build to extend the functionality of their core business system; the purchase of a stand-alone accounting package, to be hosted on new in-house infrastructure; and the purchase of a subscription to use a cloud accounting service.

The favoured option of the software engineers within the team is that of a bespoke build that extends the functionality of the core business system to include accounting capabilities they require. This approach has several benefits in that accounting software will use the strategic architecture of the core system, it will be fully integrated with other business functionality and deliver a cohesive business proposition, and, as the system will be hosted in-house, there is a high level of confidence that the accounting data will be secure. The estimated cost of building the additional functionality is £150,000 and as this sits alongside the existing functionality, the increase in ongoing maintenance will be minimal. For the sake of fair comparison, the proportion of the hosting cost allocated to this additional functionality is estimated at £2,000 per annum.

The option favoured by the company accountant is the purchase of a proprietary stand-alone package. This is largely due to them having used this package previously, however this is not to say this option does not have merit in other respects. The installation cost will be low, in comparison to a bespoke build, the costs of the stand-alone option resulting from the legal due diligence required when working with a third party and the cost of implementation and user acceptance testing. In addition to this, as the service will be hosted in-house, there are no concerns regarding data security. Current quotations and estimates put the initial costs of introducing the system at £20,000. The ongoing costs for in-house hosting and licensing fees are £20,000 per annum.

Finally, we have the option favoured by the company's finance director, namely the use of a cloud-based accounting service. Of the three options this appears to be the most economical with respect to both initial outlay and ongoing licence fees. There is, however, a perception among other stakeholders, rightly or wrongly, that hosting accounting data in the cloud has data security implications. The cost of implementing the cloud solution is estimated at £10,000 with the ongoing charges coming in at £15,000 per annum.

The following calculation uses Green Point Analysis to provide quantitative assessment of the three options:

i)   Calculate Whole Life Cost

Whole Life Cost = Build Cost + Maintenance Cost

	Build Cost	Maintenance Cost	Whole Life Cost
Bespoke Build	£150,000	£2,000 x 3	£156,000
Bought Package	£20,000	£20,000 x 3	£80,000
Cloud Service	£10,000	£15,000 x 3	£55,000

ii)   Calculate Green Points

Given that this is a new implementation, many of the parameters used to calculate green points take the same values across the options. These are listed below:

Number of Technologies, $n_t = 1$
(May differ across options but not considered)

Maintenance Life, $t_m = 36$ months

Supported Transaction Rate, $r_s = 100,000$ transactions per month

Recovered Transaction Rate, $r_r = 0$
(Assume new systems have no outages)

The main difference between options is seen on the weighting coefficients. Note, the range of weighting coefficient values used here is that quoted in Chapter 6:

	Tiering Coefficient C_T	Refactoring Coefficient C_R	Architecture Coefficient C_A	Strategy Coefficient C_S	Security Coefficient C_C	Outage Coefficient C_O
Bespoke Build	Tier 0	None	On	Strong	Minor Fix	Within Limits
	1.0	1.0	1.0	1.25	1.3	1
Bought Package	Tier 0	None	Move From	Reasonable	Minor Fix	Within Limits
	1.0	1.0	0.5	1.1	1.3	1
Cloud Service	Tier 0	None	Move From	Weak	No Fixes	Within Limits
	1.0	1.0	0.5	1.05	1.0	1

The following points are worth noting:

- The tiering coefficient is consistent across the options as this relates to the service being provided not the system providing it. It's a subtle nuance. With the service being financial, a Tier 0 classification seems appropriate; however as all options are scored the same this will not affect the comparison between them.

- Both the refactoring and outage coefficients are set to 1 as you wouldn't expect any issues with a new system in either of these respects.

- Both the Bought Package and the Cloud Service are penalised by the architecture coefficient. This is to reflect the diversification of the system estate that both of these options will cause.

- With respect to strategy coefficient, the bespoke build performs well in that it results in a cohesive and connected proposition across the business. The bought package outscores the cloud service on business strategy as it is favoured by the accounting area of the business.

- Finally, we have the security coefficient scored to reflect 'Minor Fixes' for both the bespoke build and the bought package. This is not to say that these solutions have vulnerabilities that will be addressed by this project, but more that they address the perception that the cloud service is less safe. This is a manipulation of the coefficient values that you might want to apply a different approach to. Ultimately what we are saying is the options involving in-house hosting score better when it comes to information security. Cloud service providers would probably argue that this should not be the case.

The number of green points claimed by each option is shown below:

	Green Points $n_{gp} = n_t\, t_m\, C_T\, C_S\, (r_s\, C_R\, C_A\, C_C + r_r\, C_O)$
Bespoke Build	4,972,500
Bought Package	2,187,900
Cloud Service	1,606,500

iii) Calculate Green Point Cost

Green Point Cost = Estimated Cost / Green Points

	Whole Life Cost	Green Points	Green Point Cost
Bespoke Build	£156,000	4,972,500	£0.031
Bought Package	£80,000	2,187,900	£0.037
Cloud Service	£55,000	1,606,500	£0.034

As can be seen from the above, although the whole life cost of the bespoke build is much higher, it performs better in terms of green point cost. Therefore, using the metric of green point cost the bespoke build would be the favoured option.

4. High-level Estimating

A management consultancy has received a request for information (RFI) from a new client. The potential commission involves the upgrade of the legacy equipment sited in four of their data halls. These upgrades will comprise installation of new hardware, including physical servers and networking equipment, operating systems, web servers, messaging technology, all of which must have support agreements from the respective supplier lasting a minimum of three years. Unfortunately, due to historically poor estate management and record-keeping, the scope of the work is unclear; however the client would still like a ballpark estimate in order that they can prepare a business case for the work and secure the necessary budget. The client is happy for the management consultancy's quotation to include caveats and an estimating tolerance.

The management consultancy has previously undertaken similar commissions for clients and over the course of a number of projects has collected metrics of green point costs for the upgrading of various genres of technologies. The consultant preparing the bid therefore asks the client if they have statistics regarding the trafficking of the system estate and the following management information has been provided to all tenderers:

Data Hall	Service Tier	Transactions Processed (Million/Month)	Service Level (%)
Gurney	0	4.50	98.5
Church	1	3.62	99.7
Neville	0	3.43	99.5
Griffin	2	2.15	97.2

The management consultant's green point cost metrics for data hall refurbishments are as follows:

Technology	Range (Million Green Points)	Green Point Cost
Physical Servers	0 to 100 100 to 200 200 to 500 500 +	£0.010 £0.009 £0.008 £0.007
Network Equipment	0 to 100 100 to 200 200 to 500 500 +	£0.008 £0.007 £0.007 £0.008
Operating Systems	0 to 100 100 to 200 200 to 500 500 +	£0.005 £0.004 £0.003 £0.003
Web Servers	0 to 100 100 to 200 200 to 500 500 +	£0.005 £0.004 £0.004 £0.003
Messaging Technology	0 to 100 100 to 200 200 to 500 500 +	£0.007 £0.006 £0.005 £0.004
Totals	0 to 100 100 to 200 200 to 500 500 +	£0.035 £0.030 £0.027 £0.025

i)   Calculate Green Points

The following parameters used in green point weighting vary across the data halls:

	Supported Transaction Rate r_s (per month)	Recovered Transaction Rate r_r (per month)	Tiering Coefficient C_T
Gurney	4,500,000	68,528	Tier 0 1.0
Church	3,620,000	10,893	Tier 1 0.8
Neville	3,430,000	17,236	Tier 0 1.0
Griffin	2,150,000	61,934	Tier 2 0.5

Note, the recovered transaction rate is extrapolated from the supported transaction rate using the service level quoted earlier.

E.g. (For Gurney) r_r = 4,500,000 x (100 - 98.5) / 98.5 = 68,528

The remaining green point calculation parameter values do not vary and include some assumptions:

Number of Technologies, n_t = 1 (Each technology calculated separately)
Maintenance Life, t_m = 36 months (From client specification)

Supported Transaction Rate, r_s (See table)
Recovered Transaction Rate, r_r (See table)

Tiering Coefficient, C_T (See table)
Refactoring Coefficient, C_R = 1.0 (None, application migrated)
Architecture Coefficient, C_A = 1.0 (Systems use strategic architecture)
Strategy Coefficient, C_S = 1.25 (Strong alignment)
Security Coefficient, C_C = 1.0 (No fixes implemented)
Outage Coefficient, C_O = 100 (All outages assumed outside limits)

The number of green points claimed by each upgrade is shown below:

	Green Points $n_{gp} = n_t\, t_m\, C_T\, C_S\, (r_s\, C_R\, C_A\, C_C + r_r\, C_O)$
Gurney	510,875,635
Church	169,533,641
Neville	231,912,814
Griffin	187,726,852

ii) Calculation Estimated Cost

Estimated Cost = Green Points x Green Point Cost

	Green Points	Green Point Cost	Estimate Cost
Gurney	510,875,635	£0.025	£12,771,891
Church	169,533,641	£0.030	£5,086,009
Neville	231,912,814	£0.027	£6,261,646
Griffin	187,726,852	£0.030	£5,631,806
		Total	£29,751,352

The high-level estimate for the upgrades is therefore £30m.

5. Audit/Investment Tracking

The head of risk and compliance of a global banking organisation requires a mechanism to demonstrate to regulators that his organisation is investing in the maintenance of its digital services. A discussion follows with the head of the service delivery and the pair decide that the number of green points delivered each year by Tier 0 and Tier 1 services would be a good metric to demonstrate the bank's ongoing commitment to maintaining its system estate.

The following table lists the projects involving Tier 0 and Tier 1 services. It includes both change projects, initiated to grow revenue (noted 'C'), and maintenance initiatives (noted 'M'). The current time is Y4, Q1:

Project Name	Service Tier	Live Date	Maintenance Life (Months)	Claimed Green Points
Internet Banking Re-arch. (C/M)	Tier 0	Y1, Q2	36	22,250,000
Print Service Upgrade (M)	Tier 1	Y1, Q3	60	1,450,000
Trading Platform Upgrade (M)	Tier 1	Y1, Q3	48	325,000
Foreign Exchange Platform (C)	Tier 0	Y1, Q4	60	2,350,000
IFA Wrap Platform (C)	Tier 1	Y2, Q1	24	250,000
FCA BI Feed (M)	Tier 0	Y2, Q3	24	1,200,000
Wealth Regulatory (C)	Tier 1	Y2, Q4	36	350,000
Voice IV (C)	Tier 1	Y3, Q2	48	720,000
POS Upgrade (M)	Tier 0	Y3, Q4	36	5,500,000
ATM Upgrade (M)	Tier 0	Y4, Q1	36	10,750,000

i)   Determine The Number Of Delivered Green Points

When it comes to audit we talk in terms of 'delivered' not 'claimed' green points. A green point is claimed at the point the project is implemented, however the benefit is delivered throughout the course of the maintenance life.

The following table converts claimed green points into delivered green points. Note, the green points are assumed to be delivered from the beginning of each quarter:

	Year 1	Year 2	Year 3	Year 4	Year 5	Year 6	Year 7
Project Name	**Delivered Green Points (millions)**						
Internet Banking Re-arch.	5.56	7.42	7.42	1.85			
Print Service Upgrade	0.15	0.29	0.29	0.29	0.29	0.15	
Trading Platform Upgrade	0.04	0.08	0.08	0.08	0.04		
Foreign Exchange Platform	0.12	0.47	0.47	0.47	0.47		
IFA Wrap Platform		0.13	0.13				
FCA BI Feed		0.30	0.60	0.30			
Wealth Regulatory		0.03	0.12	0.12	0.09		
Voice IV			0.14	0.18	0.18	0.18	0.05
POS Upgrade			0.46	1.83	1.83	1.38	
ATM Upgrade				3.58	3.58	3.58	
Totals	5.87	8.71	9.69	8.71	6.48	5.64	0.05

An aspect of note with the above is the IFA Wrap Platform not delivering any green points in the current year, Year 4. If the data is correct then the inference is that this system is out of support.

ii)   Present Delivered Green Points Over Time

A graphical representation of the delivered green points is shown below:

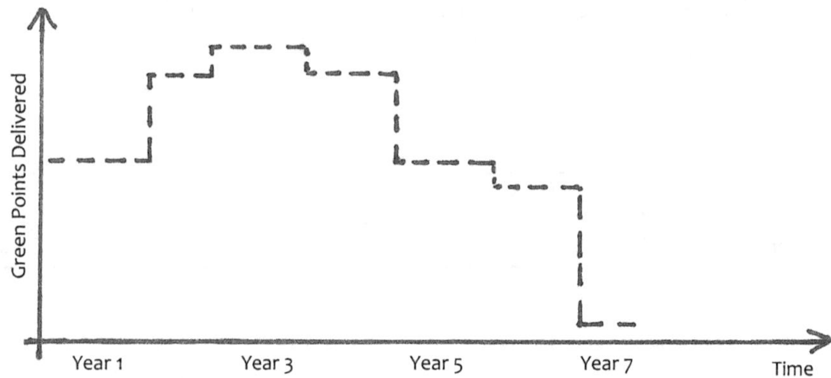

Green Point Delivery Audit Tracker

Appendix D: Transaction Estimation

T-shirt Sizing Of Transactions

Green Point Analysis is useful at the very start of maintenance activities, both during project initiation and in early analysis. If at this point you do not have a full understanding of the number of transactions a system is processing, it will be useful to have a way to estimate this.

An estimating technique that can help with this is that of T-shirt sizing. In the version of the technique described here a system is sized depending on a rough estimate of the number of users it supports. These sizes are expressed in T-shirt sizes starting at XS, for extra small, and stepping up to XXXL, extra extra extra large. Each of these sizes is then assigned an approximate number of users. The assumption here is a system will either support internal or external customers and these numbers should be well known, at least at high level. The first part of this technique is as simple as selecting the T-shirt that approximates to this number of users. The knowledge of your user base should be good enough to lead you to the appropriate size.

Another input to this technique involves consideration of a typical user's usage pattern: does a typical user access or interact with the system hourly, daily, weekly? Once you have decided on these two features of a system's usage and the number of transactions generated during a typical system use, it's simple to estimate the approximate total number of transactions that the system will be required to process. Note, the transactions here are business transactions resulting from user interactions. No consideration is made for system-generated batch transactions.

T-shirt Sizing Example

The following example shows how T-shirt sizing may be used to estimate the transactions processed by a staff-facing system with 120 users. Users generally log on to the system most days and a typical user session generates about 50 transactions.

Number of Users	
XS	100
S	500
M	5,000
L	20,000
XL	50,000
XXL	100,000
XXXL	250,000

Typical Usage Factor	
Hourly	1,820
Daily	260
Weekly	4
Monthly	1
Annually	0.1

Note, the user numbers shown here are for example purposes only and may vary by organisation and business domain.

Number of Users (XS) = 100
Typical Usage Factor (Daily) = 260
Transactions per Session = 50
Transactions
= Number of Users x Typical Usage Factor x Transactions per Session
= 100 x 260 x 50 = 1,300,000 transactions per year

Appendix E: Other Weighting Coefficients

Depending on the type of organisation you work for and the business domain in which it operates, there may be other considerations you wish to include in your Green Point Analysis. The six weighting coefficients listed above do not represent an exclusive or comprehensive list. Some other possibilities for weighting coefficients are listed below. These other options can be used to replace one or more of the coefficients mentioned previously, or they could be used alongside them. The important thing to avoid is double counting. This occurs when two or more coefficients express what is essentially the same consideration.

As mentioned previously, with regard to deciding on the coefficients you will use and the range of values they may take, it is a good idea to pick a few of your current projects, plug in some numbers and see what works for you. If you included others with competing views in this decision, then you will be able to agree an approach that accommodates competing priorities.

Support Level Coefficient

Throughout the course of this book we have assumed system support to be binary and a system to be either in or out of support. In practice this may not be the case. It may be that, in order to extend the maintenance life of a system, an organisation purchases an extended support licence. In this scenario the support provided by the vendor may be of a lesser service level than the full support level. That is to say that the guaranteed response times once an issue is raised may be longer and any guarantees regarding the remedies of an issue will be less onerous. If this is the case it may be useful to apply a support level coefficient to reduce the number of any green points claimed during an extended support period.

By way of an example, consider a scenario where a system is nearing the end of its maintenance life. It may be that the options available include a strategical approach, in which a full upgrade is performed, and a technical solution involving the purchase of an extended support licence. If it is the case that the extended support licence leads to a reduction in vendor support levels, then the green points claimed throughout the course of the extended maintenance life should reflect this. This can be done by applying a support level coefficient.

Normalising Coefficient

Ideally the type of transactions you use in your Green Point Analysis will be consistent across the piece. If this is not possible and you have to use more than one, then you need a way of aligning their respective importance. For example, you may be considering the maintenance of two systems: the first a brochureware site used to present the marketing literature that drives sales, and the other a sales system that processes the financial transactions. In this scenario there is no candidate transaction that appears on both platforms, with the former supporting read-only page impressions, and the latter the processing of retail transactions.

What is needed is a way to reflect the relative importance of these two types of transactions. Given that these two systems work in conjunction, with the brochureware site driving sales into the sales system, this is not easy. For the sake of this discussion let's assume the financial transactions take precedence. This is perhaps not a bad assumption in that the brochureware site serves as a gateway to the sales system, so if something isn't working it might as well be this. A working brochureware site driving sales to a broken sales system would be a waste of the customer's time.

If it is the financial transactions that take priority, then a normalising coefficient can be used to diminish the effect of the brochureware site's page impressions on the green point calculation point. It may be that the normalising coefficient takes the value of 1.0 for the financial transactions, and 0.1 for page impressions, the result being that the significance of financial transactions is increased ten-fold.

Exaggerating the impact of a financial transaction by ten times will not, however, make a great deal of difference if the volume of page impressions served by the brochureware site is such that this exaggeration is negated. At the very least the normalising coefficient should equalise the respective traffic levels. If you then wish to favour a particular type of transaction you need to calibrate your normalising coefficient accordingly.

Regulatory Coefficient

A regulatory coefficient will serve to represent the requirement of external stakeholders, such as regulators, ombudsmen, industry bodies and accreditors. If a particular system is vital to a relationship external to your organisation, then you may wish to reflect this in your Green Point Analysis.

There are a couple of things to mention with respect to regulatory coefficients. Firstly, you need to be careful not to double count. It could be that the tiering and strategy coefficients already account for obligations the company has to external bodies. To further exaggerate this would be at the expense of systems that may not satisfy a regulatory requirement but are still crucial to the commercial viability of the organisation. The other thing to consider is the possibility of override. It may well be that conforming to regulatory requirements takes precedence over all other considerations, and that projects that include a regulatory impact will be progressed regardless of their priority expressed by green points claimed. That is not to say Green Point Analysis should not be performed. It may be useful to know how many green points a regulatory project claims from a tracking perspective and regulatory projects themselves may need to be prioritised against each other.

Full Support Coefficient

Green points can be claimed by upgrading technologies in isolation. Indeed, there may be economies of scale in upgrading a particular technology across the whole system estate. From a single system perspective there is value in doing this as the likelihood of a failure in the upgraded component will reduce. There is still, however, a risk that one of the other components in need of an upgrade may fail and bring down the whole system. With this considered you may wish to award additional green points to a maintenance initiative which brings the whole system under support and consequently eliminates any weak links. Effectively, a bonus is being awarded for completing the job.

If you are tasked with updating a system estate one technology at a time, it is likely that all technologies do not feature on all systems. There may therefore be some benefits to be found in the order in which these technologies are upgraded, i.e. the approach you take may serve to bring more systems into full support sooner. The use of a full support coefficient will allow you to factor this into your deliberations.

Service Level Coefficient

Whereas a tiering coefficient may be used to reflect the importance of transactions from a business perspective, a service level coefficient could be used to recognise agreements internal to the organisation. It is not unusual for those tasked with operating and maintaining systems to form a service level agreement with those using the systems to conduct business. It may therefore make sense to skew the direction of maintenance effort in the direction of those services with more onerous service level requirements. In doing so we are supporting an assumption that higher levels of service require greater levels of maintenance.

It should be noted that the use of a service level coefficient has the potential for double counting. It could well be that the service level agreement reflects obligations already accommodated by the tiering coefficient.

Functional Complexity Coefficient

Although similar to Green Point Analysis in that it provides a unit of measure, Function Point Analysis (FPA) has a different focus. Whereas FPA is concerned with the amount of business functionality comprising a system, Green Point Analysis relates to the level to which the functionality is used. The most complex functionality known to man could not claim any green points if a transaction were not passed through it. As somewhat of a side effect, Green Point Analysis recognises that there are large swathes of code out there that are rarely used.

If we haven't convinced you that functional complexity is not something you need to worry about then you can, if you insist, include a functional complexity coefficient in your Green Point Analysis. In doing so you could claim more green points maintaining complex systems than you would more simple ones. In order to do this, you could call upon FPA and determine a system's size in function points, or alternatively you could perform a subjective assessment of system complexity and apply a ranking of high, medium or low. The latter would seem more in keeping with the general application of Green Point Analysis.

Hardware Coefficient

When it comes to understanding the size of a maintenance project, the amount of hardware involved should be a key consideration. It will take longer to build six physical servers as opposed to two and there is more effort involved and more scope for issues when more deployments are performed. You could therefore argue that the amount of hardware involved in a maintenance initiative should be reflected in the claiming of green points. The way to do this would be to introduce a hardware coefficient to reflect the amount of kit involved. There is no issue with this; however you do need to remember that the quantity of hardware is generally a function of the amount of traffic it is being asked to support, and consequently this may be reflected in the number of transactions a system is processing. It is therefore important to consider whether the inclusion of a hardware coefficient will lead to double counting and the artificial inflation of the green points claimed.

What we are saying here is that if you have six servers then each one is only hosting a sixth of the traffic, so if you multiply your green point count by six to reflect the number of servers you are maintaining, you should also divide your transactions by six to reflect each server is only processing its share.

Running Cost Coefficient

Whether you are implementing a new system or upgrading an existing one it is important to consider the ongoing cost of running a system. With respect to maintenance activity, it may be that the implementation of an upgrade presents a saving in running costs. The licensing costs of newer technologies could be lower, or you might be utilising a cheaper architecture, for example by moving from dedicated physical to virtual servers.

If the reduction in ongoing costs is an outcome of your maintenance work, then a running cost coefficient could be used to reflect cost savings in the number of green points claimed. If you do decide to do this there are a couple things to note. Firstly, when calculating system costs, it is best to work with whole life cost and consider both the capital outlay involved in the upgrade alongside the running cost for the maintenance life of the system you are upgrading. You also need to think about double counting as cost savings achieved by moving to a more strategic architecture may have been accounted for by the architecture coefficient.

Revenue Coefficient

With few exceptions we are all in business to make money. Therefore, you may wish to factor in the amount of revenue a system generates into your Green Point Analysis and consequently the number of green points its maintenance claims. If you do wish to reflect revenue in your Green Point Analysis then a revenue coefficient can be used.

Appendix F: Frequently Asked Questions

When should green points be calculated?

Green Point Analysis can be used throughout the project/programme life cycle. It may also be applied after project implementation in the analysis of historical data. If applied early on, at project inception, planning assumptions may need to be made with respect to the parameters used in green point calculation. Note, if Green Point Analysis is to be used in comparisons, such as those which may be performed on historical data to produce performance metrics, then it must be applied consistently.

What can be done if the number of transactions is unknown?

The number of transactions processed by a system is a key input to Green Point Analysis and the calculation of green points. In cases where the number of transactions is not known, an estimate can be determined using the T-shirt sizing method described in Appendix D.

Why is the number of items of hardware (e.g. servers) not considered?

There is an expectation that the level of hardware provision will correlate to the number of transactions processed by the service; consequently the number of hardware items is not explicitly considered. The removal of the need to know how much hardware is involved allows Green Point Analysis to be applied much earlier in the project life cycle.

Organisations that have a real need to consider hardware items could include a hardware complexity weighting coefficient in their Green Point Analysis.

Why is whole life cost used in financial assessments?

Whole life cost (i.e. the capital cost of the project plus the operational expense incurred throughout the course of the maintenance life) is used in order that changes to operational costs resulting from maintenance activities are considered. An example where this would be relevant is when a service is moving from a dedicated physical to a consolidated virtual environment.

Are regulatory initiatives reflected in Green Point Analysis?

It is not expected that maintenance initiatives will be prioritised solely on the basis of Green Point Analysis, and regulatory commitments will take precedence. The regulatory nature of a system will, however, be reflected by the tiering coefficient and, more than likely, the strategy coefficient. That is not to say a regulatory coefficient cannot be used. This is discussed in the Tiering Coefficient section of Chapter 6 and in Appendix E under Regulatory Coefficient.

How is the maintenance life calculated when more than one technology is being upgraded?
Green Point Analysis can be performed on each technology upgraded and then totalled to demonstrate the green points claimed by the whole maintenance initiative. It may, however, be simpler to view the initiative as a whole. In this case the shortest maintenance life should be used in the calculation of green points, to give a conservative total.

Can change initiatives claim green points?
If an initiative leads to the extension of a service's maintenance life, then it can be seen as claiming green points. It should, however, be noted that when the introduction of a new system leads to the decommissioning of a legacy system, then the start of the new system's maintenance life coincides with the end of the maintenance life of the legacy system.

Appendix G: Glossary of Terms

Burn Rate: A measure of how fast the programme or project budget is being spent.

Claiming Green Points: Green points are claimed at the point the maintenance or remediation initiative project is implemented.

Delivering Green Points: Green points are delivered throughout the course of the system's maintenance life, i.e. when the associated transactions are processed.

Function Point Analysis (FPA): A method to deliver a metric or unit of measurement to express the amount of business functionality an information system provides to the user.

Green Point: A metric or unit of measurement used to express the value embedded by the maintenance and remediation of information systems, based on the transactions they process and the business value of those transactions exaggerated or diminished by the application of one or more weighting coefficients.

Green Point Analysis: A method for quantifying the value gained from maintenance and remediation activities undertaken to upgrade the middleware, infrastructure and the non-functional aspect of application software.

Green Point Cost: The financial cost of claiming a green point, i.e. the estimated whole life cost of an initiative divided by the number of green points it can claim.

Green Point Rate: The time taken to undertake the work required to claim a green point. Green points are claimed at the time the work is implemented.

Gold-plating: Completing more work than is required by the agreed scope of a programme or project.

Health Lens: A characteristic of a system that when examined provides an assessment of a particular aspect of a system's health.

Maintenance Life: The extension to the support period provided by system maintenance and remediation activities.

Recovered Transaction: A transaction that will run on supported technology, which would have been lost due to an outage if it were not for system maintenance.

Software Stack: The collection of software components or computer programs an information system is comprised of, including operating systems, middleware (such as servers, content management systems and messaging technology) and applications.

Supported Transaction: A transaction that will run on supported technology as a result of system maintenance.

System Estate: The collection of information systems used by an organisation to support its internally and externally facing business activities.

Weighting Coefficient: A multiplying factor applied to a transaction to exaggerate or diminish its relative importance. A green point is calculated by applying one or more weighting coefficients to a transaction.

Whole Life Cost: The capital cost of the project plus the operational expense incurred throughout the course of the system's maintenance life.